AF809072

Entrepreneurs: The Economic Spark

Thomas Metz

Bettencourt

Bettencourt Publishing Ltd.

Copyright © 2025 Thomas V. Metz, Jr.
All rights reserved.

Published by Bettencourt Publishing Ltd., Bend, Oregon
www.bettencourtpub.com
First Edition, 2025

No part of this publication may be reproduced, stored in a retrieval system, or transmitted in any form or by any means, electronic, mechanical, photocopying, recording, scanning, or otherwise, except as permitted under the U.S. Copyright Act, without either the prior written permission of the Publisher, or authorization through payment of the appropriate per-copy fee to the Copyright Clearance Center.

Library of Congress Cataloging-in-Publication Data:

Metz, Thomas V., 1951-
Entrepreneurs: The Economic Spark
Thomas V. Metz, Jr.
p. cm. -- (Bettencourt Finance Series)
Includes index.
ISBN: 978-0-9898398-6-0
1. Business Entrepreneurship. 2. Economics. I. Title.

Printed in the United States of America

10 9 8 7 6 5 4 3 2 1

Also by Thomas Metz

Selling the Intangible Company—How to Negotiate & Capture the Value of a Growth Firm

Perfect Your Exit Strategy—7 Steps to Maximum Value

Defining Excellence—The Discipline of Company Definition

DEDICATION

This book is dedicated to America's entrepreneurs. Thank you for creating all of our companies, all of our jobs and all of our innovation.

CONTENTS

INTRODUCTION

Entrepreneurs are the spark of the economy. They create companies, jobs and the innovative products and services that make our lives better. Operating in free markets, entrepreneurs have brought Americans the highest standard of living in the world.

The most important thing that entrepreneurs do is create value. This value can be new products, new services and new ways of doing things more efficiently.

When starting and building their companies, entrepreneurs must take risks despite the possibility of failure. They don't expect to fail, but failure is always a possibility.

For entrepreneurs to be successful—to grow, to create innovative products, to employ people and pay higher wages—they must operate in an environment of economic freedom. Economic freedom means that people are free to produce and trade with others. They can control their own labor and property, free from coercion or compulsion. Individuals can work, produce, consume and invest however they choose.

Entrepreneurs actually create the demand for their products. That is where demand comes from. Production is what truly drives the economy—not spending, not consumption and not demand.

Profits are widely misunderstood and much smaller than people realize. Profits are the foundation for growth and generating new jobs. Profits lead to higher wages and surprisingly, lower prices.

The second part of the book explores the market dynamics that are the foundation of our economy. Markets and competition improve quality, lower prices, boost wages and expand consumer choice. Investment powers this entire system. Growth and innovation are the forces that bring us new medicines, healthier foods, safer automobiles and new forms of entertainment.

Part three debunks three common myths and misconceptions about how the economy works. For instance, many believe the economy behaves like a machine. Not true. The economy is constantly evolving—it's an ecosystem in which each part affects the others.

The economy is not a fixed pie or a zero-sum activity. One person's success does not come at the expense of another person. A third myth is that printing money boosts the economy. We visit Robinson Crusoe's island to discover why this is not true.

Part four addresses the bigger questions about why the United States economy has been so successful. Is it our rich natural resources? Our smart, educated people? Our strong work ethic? Is it access to capital or rule of law? The answers may be different than you think. This section also examines the culture of risk-taking that makes America unique.

The nature of opportunity is widely misunderstood. What does opportunity really mean? This chapter also explores the notion of equality. There are two distinct aspects of equality: equality of outcome and equality of opportunity. The chapter examines the relationship between these concepts.

Musings on Capitalism is the final chapter. It examines the nature of free market capitalism and how it plays out in the real world. The chapter discusses concepts like customer sovereignty—how customers determine which businesses succeed—and the importance of innovation. Capitalism's greatest benefit is that it creates wealth, reduces poverty and creates opportunity. The chapter concludes with the strong moral case for capitalism.

Entrepreneurs are fascinating. What makes them tick? What types of personalities are entrepreneurs? Why do they succeed? Entrepreneurs come in all sizes and shapes. Some are extroverts, others introverts; some are quiet, others are bold and outspoken. They share common traits: tenacity, resilience and they never give up. Appendix A digs into these personalities.

The remaining appendices explore some interesting aspects of our free market system. Why do we need Wall Street? Why do we have corporations? In addition, they examine the measurable factors that determine economic freedom. Finally, they address key technology questions: Do robots reduce employment? How will artificial intelligence affect job creation and how can entrepreneurs harness the capabilities of AI to build companies?

The American economy is exceptional. We need to understand the foundations that make this amazing process work. Economic literacy matters. The policies we vote for and the regulations we pass have real consequences for people and businesses—we need to understand those effects. This book helps Americans understand the basics about our free market system.

A Front Row Seat

I have had a front row seat on entrepreneurship for decades. My understanding comes from 42 years in business as an entrepreneur myself. I founded a boutique investment banking firm specializing in mergers and acquisitions of technology companies. My clients were across the United States (and several in Europe), and every one was an entrepreneur. I have met hundreds of entrepreneurs.

Before founding my firm, I worked for several entrepreneurial companies, most notably DeLorean Motor Company. John DeLorean hired me fresh out of business school. The company's failure was unfortunate. With better management, it could have succeeded; there was an ample market for a unique, high-end automobile. That experience taught me just how difficult building a successful business really is.

My father was also an entrepreneur and inventor/engineer. I witnessed both his successes and struggles firsthand. These experiences have convinced me that entrepreneurs taking risks in free markets are the true drivers of all economic growth.

Entrepreneurs: The Economic Spark

PART I. Entrepreneurs in Action

1 THE DRIVERS OF CHANGE

Entrepreneurs launch companies and create jobs while developing innovative products and services that transform our lives. These innovators are among America's greatest resources.

In the process of building companies, these business founders take risks and solve problems. They are determined and dogged. Many fail and a few succeed, but these are the people who make things happen.

What is an Entrepreneur?

The word "entrepreneur" derives from the French word "entreprendre," that means "to undertake." This is exactly what entrepreneurs do—they undertake new ventures and create businesses from the ground up.

Being an entrepreneur is not a traditional profession like being a teacher, or lawyer or hospital administrator. Entrepreneurs do not follow the normal path—they create entirely new paths.

Entrepreneurship can take many forms. Some entrepreneurs launch a software or technology company, some open a restaurant and others may start a trucking business. The common thread is their willingness to step into uncertainty and create something new.

ENTREPRENEURS START ALL THE COMPANIES

Every company in the United States was started by an entrepreneur who had initiative and the determination to build a business. The Fortune 500 exists because 500 entrepreneurs took risks and persevered.

Today there are 33 million businesses operating in the United States, Most are one-person firms and 6 million business have one or more employees[1]. Every one was launched by an entrepreneur who had the courage to start something new.

Image by Vika Glitter from Pixabay

Entrepreneurs create companies across a wide variety of industries. DoorDash was built by Tony Xu into a successful food delivery business after early years of struggle. Sara Blakely founded Spanx. Reed Hastings started Netflix.

Oren and Nancy Dobronsky opened Oren's Hummus, an authentic Israeli restaurant in Palo Alto. They partnered with restaurant consultant Mistie Cohen and her chef husband, David, and now have restaurants

[1] Forbes, Top Small Business Statistics, www.forbes.com/advisor/business/small-business-statistics/

across the Bay Area. Maxim Lobovsky, David Cranor and Natan Linder met at MIT and founded Formlabs. The company produces 3D printing tools for engineers, manufacturers and product designers. Despite their different industries, the common thread among these entrepreneurs is the willingness to risk time and money on an unproven idea.

Entrepreneurs are responsible for the ecosystems that develop around their businesses. When an entrepreneur starts a company, it creates opportunities for suppliers, distributors, service providers and other supporting businesses.

Image by Joenomias from Pixabay

When the founders launched Uber, new opportunities emerged in related fields to serve ride-share drivers: background check services and insurance products for commercial driving. Car rental companies developed programs for aspiring Uber drivers without cars. Food delivery businesses like DoorDash and Grubhub used the Uber model to create new markets. Most importantly, millions of drivers became micro-entrepreneurs.

As Tesla grew, the company sparked opportunities for new industries to develop. Panasonic invested billions to build a factory to produce lithium-ion batteries for Tesla. ChargePoint and Electrify America raised significant capital to build thousands of charging stations across the country. Auto suppliers retooled their operations to manufacture electric vehicle components like battery management systems instead of traditional car parts.

Let's Do it Again!

Successful entrepreneurs often create multiple companies throughout their careers. Richard Branson is an excellent example. His first venture was a magazine, then he started a mail-order record business, record stores and then a music label, Virgin Records. He went on to launch Virgin Atlantic, Virgin Mobile, Virgin Galactic and others. Not every business was a success. Failures include Virgin Cola, Virgin Cars, Virgin Clothing and others. Branson enjoys the challenge of building a business and he has an exceptional competence in promoting his brands. Today the Virgin Group operates in 35 countries and employes more than 60,000 people[2].

Why do entrepreneurs start multiple companies? Many are quite creative, like artists, and have lots of ideas. Just because you painted the Mona Lisa doesn't mean you stop painting. Creative people do not have just one idea.

Once a company is established and running smoothly, many entrepreneurs get restless or bored. They want the challenge of building something new again. Entrepreneurs who have focused intensely on a specific market often spot other gaps or unmet needs. They have learned many skills—how to hire, raise money, get customers, build a brand. In addition, if they were successful, they likely have some capital to invest.

I can tell you for certain that the entrepreneur made a number of painful mistakes in their first venture that they vow never to make again. They want to give it another go.

ENTREPRENEURS CREATE JOBS

Every private sector job in the United States originates from the initiative of an entrepreneur. *Every job.* Even

---

[2] Leaders, https://leaders.com/rankings/person/richard-branson/

government jobs are paid for by tax revenues generated by people and companies in the private sector.

A job is created because a business has some work that needs to be done. Perhaps they need an additional truck driver or another engineer. A business can serve its customers better with the right team of people. The decision to hire is made by the entrepreneur, business owner or by a manager.

Hiring a new salesperson is a good example. The more salespeople a business has, the greater likelihood of acquiring new customers. If it hires engineers, it can develop new and better products. By hiring a customer service person, the business can do a better job of keeping customers happy. It is in a company's self-interest to hire enough good people to keep the business running smoothly and effectively. To illustrate how entrepreneurs create jobs, let's look at two real-world examples.

Jobs at Schwab

Charles Schwab started his stock brokerage company in 1974. He launched the business with four employees and a personal loan on his house. Today the company provides a wide range of financial services. It employs 32,000 people and has 36 million customer accounts. The company's stock is publicly traded and it has a market value of $160 billion.

Over 50 years, the company has grown from five people to 32,000 people. That is how jobs and value are created. All because Chuck wanted to have his own business.

Image by sergeitokmakov from Pixabay

Stripe Jobs

Stripe simplifies the payment process for businesses that accept payments online. The company has created more than 8,500 jobs—good jobs, especially for engineers. The firm is one of the highest paying tech companies and provides excellent benefits. Stripe also offers stock options for its employees, providing another form of compensation beyond generous salaries. Later, Chapter 3 explores how Stripe creates value.

Stripe's growth illustrates an important point about job creation. There is a widespread myth that "demand creates jobs." This is not true in the slightest. The phrase implies that there is no decision on the part of the entrepreneur or business owner. In other words, that there is no risk.

Speaking as a business owner who has hired people, I can tell you that there is always a risk when hiring. What if we don't have enough work for them? How will we pay them if business does not pick up? Do we have enough cash to pay them going forward? These are real questions that confront business owners. Jobs are created by entrepreneurs and businesses, not by demand. Chapter 4 examines demand in more depth.

The reverse is also true. Companies that are not growing don't need to hire additional people. In fact, they are likely to lay people off because they may not have enough work for them to do. The company may be losing money and not have sufficient cash to meet payroll.

ENTREPRENEURS INNOVATE

Entrepreneurs are responsible for creating all the innovative products and services that we enjoy. What new products or services do you use today that were invented in the last five years? There are probably more than you realize. Let's look at several examples of novel products developed by entrepreneurs.

Redwood Materials

Electric cars are the fastest-growing sector of the automobile business. There are two problems with the electric vehicle business—recycling the old batteries and sourcing the specialty metals needed to produce new batteries. Redwood Materials solves both problems.

Redwood's sophisticated hydrometallurgy process extracts cobalt, lithium and nickel from used batteries. These critical components are then processed into materials for new batteries. Redwood's approach consumes less energy, generates fewer CO2 emissions and uses less water than traditional methods. The company achieves a 95% recovery rate for critical materials. This is exceptional efficiency in recycling.

Apeel Sciences

James Rogers invented a new way to preserve fruits and vegetables. His company, Apeel Sciences, developed technology that extends the shelf life of fresh produce. The product is a thin coating, derived from plants, that slows oxidation and reduces water loss. The coating is applied to fruits and vegetables such as avocados, cucumbers, citrus fruits and other produce. This natural protection reduces food waste in developing countries that lack refrigeration infrastructure.

Image by JohnyVid from Pixabay

Customers include farmers and growers who purchase the coating powder and the equipment for applying it. Rogers also provides a service team to install it. Rogers turned his innovation into a thriving business that tackles global food waste.

When entrepreneurs build successful companies, they create wealth that did not exist before. Charles Schwab's company is worth $160 billion today—wealth that exists because Chuck took a risk in 1974. Stripe is valued at $90 billion—value created by the Collison brothers' payment innovation. This is not wealth taken from someone else, it's new wealth created from ideas and hard work.

What types of people are entrepreneurs? Entrepreneurs come from all backgrounds and all personality types. Anyone can be an entrepreneur—there are no entrance exams or required degrees. But entrepreneurship is not for the faint of heart. It takes courage to make sales calls, hire and fire people, and face daily obstacles like cash flow problems. They see opportunities where others see obstacles and take action.

The four essential traits are explained in Appendix A, but here's a hint—the quintessential quality of every successful entrepreneur is determination, relentless determination.

Can entrepreneurship be taught? Many colleges offer classes in entrepreneurship. This is a good thing—but that does not create entrepreneurs. Determination is not something one learns in business school.

Appreciating Entrepreneurs

We owe a debt of gratitude to entrepreneurs. They take on difficult tasks, blaze new trails and build the companies that employ us all. Many fail, but those who succeed make our lives better. Fortunately, America has a culture that embraces entrepreneurs and risk-taking—one of our greatest economic strengths.

2 THE VALUE CREATORS

Look around you. The smartphone in your hand, the coffee maker on your counter, the car in your driveway—entrepreneurs created all of these. Someone took a risk, started a business and made your life easier. Tasks that took hours a generation ago now take seconds.

Each of these things represents the creation of value. Value is simple: anything people willingly pay for because it improves their lives, solves their problems or brings them joy. When someone hands over their hard-earned money, they're deciding—this is worth more to me than my cash.

People find value across a wide spectrum. There is value in the app that helps you navigate traffic, the investment platform that grows your retirement savings or the surgery that repairs a torn ACL.

People also appreciate things that are not actually useful. For example, someone might enjoy a nice painting. It is not as useful as a microwave oven, but it is beautiful nonetheless and people value it.

Value is subjective. No government bureaucrat could possibly know that you'll pay $5 for coffee while your neighbor won't pay $2, or that one person treasures a vintage guitar while another sees junk. This subjective nature of value is why free markets work so well—they allow individual preferences to play out.

How is Value Created?

Creating value means producing goods and services that solve problems or improve lives. It happens at every level—from a teenager mowing lawns to Elon Musk building rockets. The mechanic who fixes your car creates value. The software developer who designs a database creates value. The inventor who designs a better medical device creates value.

Value exists even without money changing hands. When you cook dinner for your family, you have created value—a nutritious meal that brings everyone together. When a farmer grows crops, he has created value. When a craftsman builds furniture for his den, he has created value. Value is about making life better, whether someone pays for it or not.

The key insight is that entrepreneurs are simply people who create value that others are willing to pay for. They take their drive to improve things and turn it into businesses that serve customers.

Derek the Deck Guy

Let's assume that that the deck on the back of your house is getting a little shabby. How much does it cost to have the deck replaced? You get several bids to rebuild the deck. You decide to hire Derek the Deck Guy for $6,500. Plus, he was highly recommended by a friend. (If you are handy with home projects, you

could build the deck yourself.) Derek builds the deck. Derek has created real value—he took wood and hardware worth maybe $2,000 and his skills turned them into a $6,500 deck.

Building a House

Now let's expand the deck example and construct a complete house. The principle is the same. The builder or general contractor will purchase concrete, wood, glass, wiring, pipes and all the other materials that go into building a house. He hires skilled craftsmen to build the house.

The average value of a house in the U.S. is $435,000. How much does it cost to build such a house?

- Land: $120,000
- Architect, plans & permits: $30,000
- Materials—wood, glass, pipe, wiring, roofing, etc.: $135,000
- Craftsmen and labor: $100,000
- General contractor fee: $50,000
    - Total costs: $435,000

The contractor organized all these pieces and created $435,000 in value. This same principle applies when entrepreneurs build companies—they organize resources to create something people want.

ENTREPRENEURS CREATE VALUE

When an entrepreneur successfully builds a company, they create real value. Let's look at several entrepreneurs who started businesses and created billions of dollars in value.

Stripe Creates Value

Stripe simplifies the payment process for merchants that accept payment from credit and debit cards. It transfers funds securely between a customer and the merchant.

Stripe is particularly effective for merchants that sell products online. Stripe's solution is much simpler than other clumsy payment systems. In addition, Stripe provides fraud detection and important security features. Customers include almost half of the Fortune 100 companies.

The company was founded in the San Francisco Bay Area in 2010 by two brothers, Patrick and John Collison. The original $2 million investment in Stripe was provided by a handful of successful entrepreneurs and three venture capital firms. Over the last 15 years Stripe has raised a great deal of investment capital, totaling about $9 billion.

Stripe has become exceptionally successful and the company is currently valued at around $90 billion. The Collison brothers identified a real problem—clunky payment systems—and built a solution that businesses desperately needed. That's $90 billion in value created by solving a problem that millions of merchants faced every day.

Apple Creates Value

Steve Jobs and Steve Wozniak created the Apple company that currently has a market value of $3.0 trillion. Jobs and Wozniak founded Apple on April 1, 1976. When they started the company, it was worth zero. It was just two guys with an idea and no assets. Over the last 49 years the value went from zero to $3.0 trillion. That is genuine wealth creation.

The shares of Apple stock are real. They are not just pieces of paper. They represent real ownership in a real company. The company has real buildings with real employees and it develops real products. Perhaps you own some shares of Apple stock, or you have a mutual fund or a retirement account that owns shares of Apple stock. These shares of stock are real value.

Everyone knows about the iPhone, but remember,

Apple created multiple categories of value. The iPod revolutionized music. Apple didn't invent tablets, but with the iPad they figured out how to make them intuitive and appealing. The Mac computer pioneered user-friendly computing.

Apple's journey was in no way a smooth ride. The company had several notable failures. The Newton personal digital assistant was a bust and the Lisa computer failed miserably. Both were expensive flops. Surprisingly, Steve Jobs quit or was fired from the company. He rejoined Apple two years later when the company was struggling. Even the most successful companies face setbacks along the way.

Image by kropekk_pl from Pixabay

Apple is one of the largest job creators in the United States with 164,000 employees[3]. The company estimates its ecosystem has created 2.9 million jobs across all 50 states[4].

Apple's value reflects the company's profits. The profits are high because Apple does an excellent job of serving its customers, inventing outstanding products and keeping expenses in line. Profits are the result of customers really appreciating the company's products, especially their iPhones.

---

[3] Statistica, www.statista.com/statistics/273439/number-of-employees-of-apple-since-2005/

[4] Information Week, www.informationweek.com/it-leadership/apple-s-500-billion-ai-investment-to-create-20-000-tech-jobs

Tesla Creates Value

Tesla was founded in 2003 by Marc Tarpenning and Martin Eberhard. Eight months later, Elon Musk invested $6.5 million. He became chairman of the board and took an active role in Tesla. The company raised $53 million two years later from venture capital investors including Google founders, Brin and Page. In 2008 Tesla raised $40 million in debt financing. That totals $100 million in financing. It takes a lot of money to start a car company.

It was a rocky road for Tesla. In 2008, the company was running low on cash and had to fire 25% of its employees. The next year the company raised more capital. By then, Elon Musk had invested $70 million of his own money. Building a car company from scratch meant facing one crisis after another.

Tesla continued to struggle. To save money, the company entered into partnerships with several companies to help with the production process. The first production vehicle, the Tesla Roadster, was a high-performance sports car based on the Lotus Elise chassis. It demonstrated that an electric car could be zippy, not just utilitarian.

In 2010 Tesla sold shares of stock to the public which raised $226 million for the company and the company's value was $2.5 billion. Tesla employed 650 people at the time.

Image by JackieLou DL from Pixabay

Let's fast forward 15 years to early 2025. Tesla produced and sold 1.8 million cars per year for the past two years. The company has created thousands of good jobs; today 140,000 people work at Tesla.

How much value has been created? The company raised $20 billion of total investment over 20 years and is now worth $1.3 trillion. The founders, Elon Musk, engineers and employees turned that investment into $1.3 trillion in just two decades.

If you had invested $10,000 at the public offering in 2010, your Tesla stock would be worth $2.9 million today.

As an aside, why didn't Ford or General Motors develop a successful electric car early on? They have been in the auto business for decades. They know a thing or two about building cars. Why couldn't they do it?

Who Benefits from Value Creation?

Who benefits from value creation? Obviously, stockholders benefit directly—founders, investors, employees and anyone who owned Apple or Tesla stock. But the benefits spread much wider. Anyone with a mutual fund, retirement account or 401K account that owns shares has benefited. Someone may have bought Tesla or Apple stock for their children's college fund or a university's endowment invested in the stock. They took a risk in buying the stock and it paid off.

Customers benefit from better products at lower prices. Tesla's success drove down electric car costs and forced other automakers to improve their electric vehicles. Apple's innovations made smartphones affordable for billions of people. Suppliers benefit from increased orders. Communities benefit from good-paying jobs and tax revenue.

The founders and early investors became wealthy or added to their wealth. Where does this money go? There are only three things that one can do with their money—spend it, invest it or give it away. A wealthy person only needs so many houses and cars, so the bulk of the gain on Tesla stock will be invested in other businesses and some will be given to charity.

The venture capital firms will reinvest their gains into

other entrepreneurial companies—biotech firms developing cancer treatments, startups creating clean energy solutions, or companies building artificial intelligence. This creates a virtuous cycle where successful value creation funds the next generation of innovations. We'll explore this wealth recycling process in more detail in Chapter 10.

Microsoft founder Bill Gates exemplifies this pattern. The Gates Foundation has given $60 billion to fight disease and poverty worldwide. This is what value creation makes possible.

WHO DECIDES WHAT THE VALUE IS?

Who decides what value is? The market does—meaning all the people buying and selling, voting with their dollars on what they are willing to pay.

Consider art auctions, where value has nothing to do with production costs. In 2019, a Claude Monet painting of haystacks sold for $110 million. The painting's value had nothing to do with how long it took Monet to create it in the 1890s. He called it "Les Meules" (it means 'the stacks'). Seven bidders competed for eight minutes until one person decided it was worth $110 million to them.

This was a new world record for the sale of an Impressionist painting. It is one of only four paintings from the haystacks series of 25 paintings to come up for sale in the last century.

Image from Sotheby's

The market

determined that painting's worth—not art critics, not government officials, but someone willing to pay $110 million for it.

Many assume that entrepreneurs simply respond to existing demand, creating products people already want. But this gets the relationship backward. The truth is far more interesting. Entrepreneurs actually *create* the demand.

3 ENTREPRENEURS CREATE THE DEMAND

Entrepreneurs create the demand for their innovations by conceiving and producing products and services that people want. Creating something useful is what generates demand for it.

Before an entrepreneur starts their company, there is no demand for that product because it has not been created yet. The entrepreneur believes people will want the product but it's unproven. The entrepreneur's belief drives them to start the company and produce the product.

WHAT IS DEMAND?

There is a lot of confusion about what demand is and how it affects the economy. First, we need to be more specific. The word demand alone is extremely vague and often misunderstood. To address this ambiguity, we should focus on 'economic demand,' which has a precise definition:

> *Economic demand refers to the willingness and ability to purchase specific goods at specific prices.*

Note that demand is related to price. This makes good sense because how much something costs obviously impacts how many units people will want or can afford to buy.

When Apple launched the iPad at $499, demand was different than it would have been at $199 or $999. Price matters. Real economic demand isn't just 'I want an iPad'—it's 'I want an iPad enough to pay $499 for it.'

To further illustrate the concept that demand depends on price, let's consider the market for e-bikes. If e-bikes cost $800, many people buy them. At $2,500, far fewer do. Price determines actual economic demand.

The relationship between price and demand makes forecasting tricky. No one knows the demand for e-bikes next year. Businesses attempt to forecast future demand so they can manufacture the correct number of e-bikes, but it's still a guess. Future demand is always unknown.

Since entrepreneurs create products before anyone wants them, they take significant risks. They must invest in equipment, inventory, facilities and personnel without knowing if customers will actually buy the products. They're betting their money on a hunch, not on proven demand.

The entrepreneur's commitment before knowing demand happens at businesses of all sizes. If a restaurant wants to add pizza to its menu, it must purchase a pizza oven, pizza pans and the necessary kitchen tools. The owners of the restaurant must come up with the money to buy these things, all before knowing if their customers will embrace their new pizza offering.

Sometimes entrepreneurs are correct in anticipating what the market might want. At other times, they are not correct and their businesses fail. We tend to remember the ones that succeed and forget about the failures. There are many failures. I explore failure in Chapter 6 because failure plays a key role in the story of economic success.

Entrepreneurial Vision

Many revolutionary products weren't responding to existing demand; entrepreneurs created it. People didn't know they "needed" smartphones until entrepreneurs created them. Before Ford's Model T, people wanted "faster horses," not automobiles. Streaming services were not demanded before Netflix pioneered them. The same pattern holds for social media platforms. Innovation precedes demand.

Entrepreneurs don't just try to satisfy existing demand. They anticipate needs people don't yet recognize and see possibilities that others don't. That's how they create products before demand exists.

Inventing the iPad Created Demand

Entrepreneurs try to anticipate what people might want. Would people want an iPad? Who knows? Steve Jobs thought they would. Maybe people are perfectly happy with their laptops, desktop computers and their phones. Why do we need an iPad? It seems like an extra-large telephone that doesn't fit in your pocket or your purse. Who would want one of those?

First, Apple had to design the product—how big should it be? What should it look like? What tasks should it handle? What tasks would it not do? What features should it have?

Image by StockSnap

Before any demand existed, Apple had to hire product designers, engineers, software developers, manufacturing specialists, marketing teams and sales staff. All these people were employed before the first iPad was sold—before there was any demand. Launching the iPad was a huge risk for the company.

Some argue that demand comes first—that Apple created the iPad because "people wanted it." But this gets causality backward. Before the iPad existed, nobody could specifically demand it. They might have vaguely wanted 'better technology' or 'easier ways to browse the internet'—but this is not economic demand, it's just saying 'people want stuff,' which is true but meaningless. People wanted the iPad only after Steve Jobs envisioned and designed it and after Apple invested many millions to produce it.

Demand results from entrepreneurs investing capital, inventing new products and services. Entrepreneurs create the demand for their products.

Demand is Not Known

One problem with the idea that demand drives the economy is that it presumes demand is known. Demand is never known. If demand were known, entrepreneurs would never have to take any risk because they would already know what people wanted. It would be a piece of cake. But entrepreneurship is difficult and risky precisely because entrepreneurs make decisions and spend money based on what they think the future market might be. It is always a gamble.

What if No One Buys?

What if a business produces a product and no one buys it? Every business takes this risk. If few buy the product, the business loses money. This is the inherent risk of entrepreneurship—taking chances on unproven ideas. This uncertainty makes entrepreneurship both challenging and vital to economic progress.

A business had better have other products that are successful or the company will fail. Success means profit.

Failure means losses and perhaps bankruptcy.

This chapter has highlighted the crucial role that entrepreneurs play in creating demand. Entrepreneurs take calculated risks based on their befief of future needs. They commit capital, time and resources before knowing if demand will materialize. People who think that demand or spending comes first have a fundamental misunderstanding of innovation and entrepreneurship. They get it backward. The production of goods and services is what truly makes the economy go. Production comes first. Production drives everything.

4 PRODUCTION DRIVES THE ECONOMY

Production creates economic growth. This chapter explains how production drives the economy—not spending, not consumption and not demand. The idea that demand or spending propels the economy is pervasive and false. That is not how it works.

Cart Before Horse

Before someone can buy something, they must have earned money. Their money comes from working. Working comes first. It is pointless to go to the store without some cash in your pocket.

You must grow tomatoes before you can eat the tomatoes or trade them for some carrots. Demand for tomatoes does not make the tomatoes grow. The first step is that Farmer John plants

Image by kie-ker at Pixabay

the seeds, tends the plants and picks the tomatoes. Only then can someone buy the tomatoes at the farmers' market and enjoy them in a nice salad. Demand did not make the tomatoes grow; Farmer John made the tomatoes grow.

No number of hungry customers staring at empty market stalls will make tomatoes appear. Only Farmer John's work creates the tomatoes.

CONSUMERS ARE PRODUCERS

Suppose you live in a small village where people make many of their own clothes and grow much of their own food. You are particularly skilled at crafting moccasins. On Saturdays you go down to the town market and trade some of your moccasins for other things that you need, like fresh vegetables and perhaps a new coat.

On this particular Saturday you stop by my booth and admire the excellent knives that I have fashioned. Your old knife is worn out so you decide to trade some moccasins for a new knife. My own moccasins have a hole in them that is getting bigger by the day. Your moccasins are just what I'm looking for so we make a trade and we are both happy.

Notice that this transaction occurred between two producers. You produced the moccasins and I produced the knife. So, we could say that you are the moccasin producer and the knife consumer and that I am the knife producer and the moccasin consumer. But what's the point of those labels? The producer and consumer are the same person.

Only producers can go to the market and make a trade. If you have not produced anything, then you cannot trade for anything. No one will trade with you. It would be like going to a store with no money.

If we fast forward to today's modern economy that uses money, the concept is exactly the same. In order to buy something, you must have money. You get money by working at your job and producing something. You could produce auto parts at a factory. You could create tasty meals at your catering company or you could write software programs. Your work creates value and you get paid for that. You are a producer.

Two Productions Come First

Image by Sajad Nori from Unsplash

Before you traded your moccasins for my knife, *two* acts of producing had to happen first. That's right—two. We both had to produce something before we could trade. Prior to our trade, (1) you sewed the moccasins and (2) I crafted the knife. We both produced products. Then we made a trade. For another example, imagine Robinson Crusoe's island with 100 shipwrecked survivors. Everyone creates things and trades with others. Beth makes fishing poles. Jim makes canoes. Dwight builds lean-tos. Which people on the island are the consumers and which people are the producers? Well, of course, this is a trick question. Everybody is a producer. They must make something before they can trade it to someone else. That's how our economy works too. Everyone must produce or they won't have the money to buy anything. No one is simply a "consumer."

A Consumer is not a Special Economic Actor

News articles proclaim that consumers are the engine that drives the economy. Many articles use the word "consumers" as if they were some distinct category of economic actors. It is interesting that they are called consumers and not just people or human beings. As I described above, a person can only consume something after they have produced and earned some money. Consumers are producers. They are not a separate type of economic actor.

If many consumers were the key to a thriving economy, then India and China would have the best economies in the world because they have so many "consumers." This is obviously not the case because China and India are very poor countries. A thriving economy is not based on having lots of consumers. Consumers are not a force that propels the economy. This is a myth. Producers drive the economy. Every economy.

If an entrepreneur is correct about their product's appeal, the company may make a profit. Profits are critical for every business because profits ensure survival. The next chapter examines some fundamental misunderstandings about what profits actually are.

5 PROFITS ARE MISUNDERSTOOD

...the Big Pile of Cash in the Back Room

Most Americans have completely wrong ideas about business profits. There is a perception out there that businesses are *extremely* profitable. This myth is so far from the truth as to be preposterous.

People have many different notions about what profits are. You hear all kinds of weird things: Are profits a rip-off? Are profits 'taking' something from others? Are they 'extracting'? Are profits evil? What about obscene profits? The concepts are all over the map.

The biggest myth is that people think profits are quite large when in reality, profits are quite small. Let's take a look at what profits really are.

What are Profits?

Profits are simply what is left over after a business pays all its expenses. Sales minus expenses equals profit. It is straightforward. Business expenses include things like salaries, rent, inventory, utilities, taxes—everything it takes to keep the doors open. After subtracting all the expenses from revenue, you end up with profit. If the expenses exceed revenue, the business loses money and may have trouble surviving.

Profits mean that the business is being smart about how it operates and is keeping its expenses in line. It is doing a good job running the business. Profit represents productive achievement and value creation.

PROFITS ARE SMALLER THAN YOU THINK

Businesses are nowhere near as profitable as people believe. Most people believe that a business makes a profit of forty cents or fifty cents for every $1 of sales. In other words, if a customer spends $100, then the business earns $45 in profit.

This is wildly wrong. The reality is that profits are ***seven cents*** for every $1 of sales. That's right, ***a lousy seven cents.***

Tell Us about Your Day...

Let's say you hop in your GM Chevy Malibu car, stop at Starbucks for a cup of coffee and then head over to Walmart to do some shopping for your kids. On the way home you fill up at the gas station and swing by the grocery store to get some food for dinner.

Those businesses would be pleased that you are shopping with them. But they are hardly raking it in. Their profit as a percent of sales is:

GM	3.2 %
Starbucks	10.3 %
Walmart	2.8 %
Chevron	9.1 %
Kroger (Ralphs, QFC, etc.)	1.8 %

When you spent $100 at Walmart, the company made $2.80 in profit. Your $4 coffee at Starbucks earned the company 41 cents in profit. If you filled your tank for $45 at a Chevron station, they earned $4.10. If you purchased $100 worth of groceries at a Kroger store, they made $1.80. The total cost of your shopping trip was $249 and the companies that you shopped at made a total profit of $9.11. That works out to a profit of less than 3.7%. For simplicity, we can round this up to 4%. Not 40%, not 50%, but 4% of the money that you spent!

These examples are large companies, but the story is the same if you shopped at small businesses. I chose these firms because, as public companies, the financial statements are available and I can see the profit percents.

It Depends on the Industry

Profitability depends on the industry. Some industries have skinny profits, like grocery stores and stores like Walmart. Other industries, like software, have relatively high profits. Do you use TurboTax? The company that makes it, Intuit, earns profits of 18% of sales. Software companies have high margins because reproducing software costs almost nothing. Even so, 18% is still far below what most people think companies earn.

By contrast, consider entertainment. Do you enjoy Disneyland and Disney movies? For every $100 that you spent at Disneyland, the company made a profit of $5.44. That profit is *below* the average of 7% for most companies.

Perceptions of Profits

Fortune magazine surveyed people several years ago to learn what people thought about profits. The average American thought that for every $1 in sales, a business earned a profit of **50 cents**. In other words, they believed profits were half of a company's sales. The correct answer is **7 cents**.[5]

The Right Answer

How does this poll compare to actual profits? New York University's Stern school tracks data on profitability. Their database of 6,000 companies shows an average profit as a percent of sales of 7.3% as of January 2025[5].

As part of my work as an investment banker, I monitor the profitability of the Fortune 500. These are America's biggest, most successful companies—and even they average just ***7.2%*** over the last seven years. To be clear: that is 7 cents for every $1 of sales. And these are the largest companies in the United States.

The average is relatively constant. In a bad year, profits average 5.5%, as they did in 2020. In very good years, profits average 9.2%, as they did in 2021.

Remember that this is the *average* for the Fortune 500. For every company that has higher profits there is another company with lower profits or with losses. If one company's profits are 16%, then another company is losing 4%. That is how averages work.

[5]https://pages.stern.nyu.edu/~adamodar/New_Home_Page/datafile/margin.html

A more recent poll by Reason-Rupe showed that the public believed profits were **36%** of sales[6]. They thought profits were $36 for every $100 of sales! This perception is way off; not even close to reality. Again, the correct figure is $7. This massive misperception persists today. Most Americans still believe companies make **36%** profit on sales, when the actual figure remains around **7%**.

Big Pile of Cash in the Back Room?

You may have read that some companies have huge piles of cash. Apple, Microsoft and Google are good examples. These firms have been enormously successful for decades and they simply don't have enough new projects in which to invest this cash. In mid-2025, Apple had cash of $65 billion, Microsoft had $75 billion and Google had $95 billion. Those are substantial piles of cash.

Microsoft and Apple are transferring much of this money back to their shareholders by paying dividends and by purchasing their own stock in the market. Shareholders who sell their shares can invest that money in other companies that *do* have projects needing investment.

Image by alirazabozdar from Pixabay

These huge tech companies are the exceptions. At the other end of the spectrum are the regular everyday businesses that are

[6] AEI, Mark Perry, "The public thinks the average company makes a 36% profit margin, which is about 5X too high," April 2, 2015, https://www.aei.org/carpe-diem/the-public-thinks-the-average-company-makes-a-36-profit-margin-which-is-about-5x-too-high/

chronically short of cash. They must pay their bills before getting paid by their customers, which is why bank loans are critical for their survival.

Cash flow is the life blood of every business. If the cash runs out, it is difficult to pay the bills. Most businesses are constantly tight on cash. Plus, their profits are relatively small so they do not accumulate much cash. Certainly, there is no big pile of cash in the back room.

WHY ARE PROFITS IMPORTANT?

Companies make profits in one and only one way—by serving their customers better than competitors do. The better job they do of satisfying those customers, the more profits they make. If a company doesn't do a good job of pleasing customers, they shop somewhere else and the company will lose money and eventually go out of business.

Profits are important for several reasons:

- Profits mean people want the products
- Profits lead to lower prices
- Profits create jobs and higher wages
- Profits prove that value is being created
- Profits enable growth and innovation
- Profits enable investment
- Profits mean the business can survive

Let's put a little more meat on these bones and explore why profits are important.

People Want the Products

The only way for a business to make a profit is to sell products that customers actually want. Profits show that customers are willing to pay their hard-earned cash for the products.

Recently I purchased some flannel sheets for $189. Yes, that is a lot of money for sheets. But I love flannel sheets. I was happy to pay the $189. The sheets are so comfy. The company probably made a nice profit selling them to me. It was a win-win transaction. Even for $189, I thought the sheets were worth every penny.

Profits Mean Lower Prices

Most businesses want to maximize profits. Here's how they do it. They need to sell more products. To sell more products, they must outperform their competitors. This means their products must be less expensive or higher quality. To produce less expensive and/or higher quality products, the company must invest in better machines and better design. The new machines produce more products per hour which reduces the costs. With lower costs, the company can reduce prices and sell more products. Selling more products means more profits. The result? The pursuit of profits drives prices down for everyone.

Many people think the exact opposite about this process. They presume that a company will make more profits if it raises prices. That pesky thing called competition changes everything.

In the absence of competition, certainly companies could raise their prices and perhaps increase profits. But with competition, the only way to make more money is to lower prices and sell more products. That is what happens in the real world because in the real world there is competition—lots of competition. We examine the beauty of competition in Chapter 8.

Profits Create Jobs

Profits are what create new jobs. Period. When a company makes money, it can afford to expand. The owners of a pizza restaurant may want to open a second restaurant across town. If they did, they would have to hire more workers. Profits enable them to employ people because they will have enough cash to pay the wages.

Think about the reverse situation for a moment. What

if a company was losing money? Would it create new jobs? Even if it wanted to hire more people, it could not afford to pay the wages and salaries. Likely, if a company is losing money, it will be laying people off. More profits mean more growth, which means more jobs.

Profits Mean Higher Wages

A business that is nicely profitable can attract the best employees by paying higher wages. Again, consider the opposite—a business that is barely profitable or losing money cannot afford to pay higher wages or give raises. It may be forced to lay people off. Profits are the opposite.

Why would a company pay higher wages just because it is profitable? The reason is because it must compete for employees with other businesses. If it wants to attract the most qualified employees, it must entice them with good wages and good benefits. Companies compete for workers and this competition is what drives up wages and salaries.

Value is Being Created

What does that mean—value is being created? It means that the value of the business increases as it effectively serves its customers. A company's stock price will go up if the business is profitable and doing a good job of running the business.

Profits reflect the creation of value. When a company earns strong profits, investors place a higher value on the stock. Companies with high profits are worth more than companies with low profits. This is what we mean by value creation.

Consider Kristen and Travis' family-owned pizza business that has been serving customers for years. If the business has been consistently profitable, there's a good chance the owners could sell the company when they retire. Without a track record of profits, the company would sell for a low price or perhaps not at all.

Profits Enable Growth

Without profits there can be no growth. Growth is essential because it improves our standard of living.

Growth requires cash. Companies can finance growth two ways. First, they can generate profits that provide cash to expand the business—develop new products, purchase inventory, build a branch office or open that pizza restaurant across town.

Most companies continually reinvest their profits into the business. They create new products and services to attract customers and keep up with competition. If they don't reinvest, their products become stale and customers go elsewhere. Clothing companies must develop new fashions. Car companies create new models with better technology and safety features. Computer companies make faster and more powerful computers. Your phone does more than your previous phone and has longer battery life because Apple and Samsung reinvest profits to improve their products. Drug companies develop amazing new cures for diseases.

The second way to obtain cash for growth is through investment. A business owner might take out a home equity loan on their house and invest that money in the company. A business might try to attract investors who can contribute capital. Without the potential for profits, a business cannot attract investors. Profits, or the expectation of profits, are critical for investment.

Profits Fuel Innovation

Profitable companies can afford to invest in research and development. Apple spends more than $20 billion annually on R&D. Without consistent profits, these investments would be impossible.

Profitable companies can afford to take risks on new technologies. Looking back at history, most major innovations came from profitable enterprises. Thomas Edison's electric light bulb emerged from his profitable telegraph business. The Wright brothers funded their aviation experiments through profits from their bicycle shop. Profits make innovation possible. Without them, companies can't afford to develop new products.

Profits Enable Investment

Profits are the return to the investors who invested cash in a company. They might have invested in a startup company to get it off the ground or they may have invested capital in a company that needed money to expand.

Why would an investor provide capital to a company that was not making a profit or that did not anticipate profits down the road? The answer is simple—they would not invest. Profits are the key to investment.

Consider this example: an investor builds a small apartment building, say one with six units. The investor builds the building because he thinks it will be a good investment for his retirement years. He hopes the rents collected will be greater than the costs of owning the building. Costs include maintenance, repairs, landscaping, property taxes, insurance and interest. The profit is the return on his investment.

Startups work the same way. If it were not for investors, entrepreneurs would have a difficult time starting their companies. Not many of them have enough capital to get off the ground. Some companies can get started on a shoestring but this is rare.

Today billions of dollars are invested in new companies. These firms conceive of all kinds of imaginative new products and services, such as Lyft and Uber. Uber has raised a staggering amount of money. Before it listed its stock publicly in 2019, Uber had raised $24 billion, primarily from venture capital firms. Lyft has raised $5 billion over 20 rounds of funding. These businesses are fast-growing and complicated. They require an enormous amount of capital to build a successful business. The expectation of profits drives this investment.

The Business Can Survive

Put bluntly, if a business does not make a profit, it will not survive very long. Companies must continually adapt and innovate. They must keep up with their competitors. Without profits, a company will not have enough cash to grow and improve.

The profit discipline is a cruel master. If a company does not earn profits, it will fail and go out of business. A profitable company gets to stay in business. It's a tough world out there.

Should They Pay Workers More?

Some believe it would be better if a company paid its workers more and earned a smaller profit. Certainly, a company that has been making nice profits will want to pay its employees higher than average wages and provide good benefits. This keeps the employees happy and reduces turnover.

Earning profits does not mean that a business is underpaying its workers. Businesses pay workers based on the market wage for a particular job. If experienced welders earn $85,000, there is no reason to pay a welder $125,000. That is not money well spent. Most companies pay the market wage when hiring someone for a specific job. If they did not pay a market wage, few people would work for that company.

If a company overpays its employees, it will have a difficult time competing with firms that do pay the market wage. They won't be able to keep their costs in line and they won't be able to keep prices low enough to compete.

Profitable companies can afford to pay competitive wages and attract top talent. Unprofitable companies eventually face cash flow problems and struggle to meet payroll.

PROFITS ARE NOT GREED

Some think profits are greed—that companies are 'taking' from customers and charging too much. They think profit is an overcharge, something extra, beyond the amount of what something should really cost. Along this line of reasoning, some people think that profits are actually bad. They think that profits mean that companies are charging us too much.

What about "Obscene Profits?

What about "obscene profits?" Are they bad? Oh boy, now we are getting serious. No, profits are not obscene. Profits are earned. Big profits are an invitation to competitors to compete with the company making those nice profits. It's like sending an engraved invitation: "Please compete with us because we are making a lot of money."

Take the case of memory chips. When these products were new, manufacturers could charge high prices, but this attracted competitors, leading to increased competition and lower prices. Today, memory chips sell for a fraction of their original cost; profit margins have dropped to normal levels.

High profits are usually short-lived. A competitor will notice and will enter the market and sell products at lower prices to gain an edge. So, profits eventually will fall.

WHAT IF THERE WERE NO PROFITS?

Without profits, there would be no additional hiring. No raises. No investment. No growth. Why would anyone invest if they could not earn a return? Without profits, Kristen and Travis could not open another pizza restaurant across town.

Losses are the Opposite

Think about the opposite situation. If a company is losing money, it means that customers don't want to buy its products. Either prices are too high, quality too low, or both. In addition, the company may be doing a poor job of managing its expenses.

Losses, or lack of profits, are destructive. There are several negative consequences of losses:

- Layoffs and fewer jobs
- No growth or expansion
- Bills go unpaid
- Protracted losses mean the company goes out of business

Losses mean that value is being destroyed.

Implications of the Profit Myth

In defense of the average person, they have no reason to know how much profits are. They don't teach it in school. Unless someone is keenly interested in business, there would be no reason to know the answer to the question. However, it is important to understand the world that we live in.

The danger here is that if Americans think that businesses earn 40% or 50% in profit rather than 7%, then these companies must be sitting on large piles of cash. If Americans think companies have loads of money, then we should vote to have them pay for more things—like higher wages, better benefits and we should definitely tax them more. The problem is that businesses make nowhere near as much money as people think. This is a dangerous misperception. It is important to get the facts straight before we make policy decisions.

Profits are radically smaller than what people think—just 7% of sales rather than the 36% most Americans believe. Yet these modest profits are responsible for remarkable benefits: they create jobs, enable higher wages, fund innovation and drive the investment that improves our lives.

The opposite of profits is failure. The next chapter discusses failure. Every entrepreneur faces the possibility of failure, and many do fail. The willingness to risk failure is what separates entrepreneurs from everyone else.

6 RISK, FAILURE AND RESILIENCE

Taking risks is essential for progress. People rarely accomplish great things by playing it safe. Entrepreneurs understand this—they're always trying new approaches, developing new products and shaking up established ways of doing business. Some ideas work, some don't, but without risk-taking there's no innovation.

The biggest risk for any entrepreneur is failure and failure is common. More than half of startup businesses fail within five years. Entrepreneurs risk their own money to build their businesses. They typically must personally guarantee bank loans and leases and often they will borrow against their homes to pay employees. For many entrepreneurs, their entire net worth is tied up in the business they're creating. If they fail, they can lose everything.

Risk-taking is underappreciated because we often don't see it. We don't notice the startup that spent four years developing a product, then quietly went out of business when it didn't work.

But customers benefit when entrepreneurs invent new products, develop new drugs or create new technologies.

The more entrepreneurs who experiment, the more breakthrough products we all get to enjoy.

A Culture of Risk-Taking

Americans start new businesses at much higher rates than people in other developed countries. We're more willing to quit stable jobs to chase new opportunities, and our legal system makes it easier to recover from business failures.

Japan exemplifies this difference. The Japanese are smart, hard-working and highly innovative in manufacturing and engineering. But they value conformity over risk-taking. Japanese companies excel at manufacturing but produce fewer breakthrough innovations.

Germany is another country whose people are intelligent and industrious, with a reputation for superior engineering. Yet their culture values planning, rules and regulations—all focused on providing a sense of security rather than encouraging risk-taking. How many German entrepreneurs have built companies that rival American tech leaders?

The cultures of these two countries emphasize collectivism over individualism. They value strong group cohesion and conformity. These characteristics lead businesses to avoid risk and uncertainty.

The United States is the opposite; our culture embraces individualism. We emphasize individual freedom and achievement over group conformity. We value fresh ideas and innovation over

following established procedures. This cultural difference isn't just interesting—it's why America produces far more breakthrough companies than any other country.

This is why we should not resent successful entrepreneurs who become wealthy. When someone like Steve Jobs or Elon Musk became rich from their innovations, they didn't take wealth from others—they created entirely new wealth that benefits everyone. Their success isn't a zero-sum game; it makes all of us better off.

This willingness to take risks and challenge established ways of doing business creates constant change in our economy. That change has a name: creative destruction.

Creative Destruction

New business models are invented and old business models become obsolete. Recent examples include:

- Netflix revolutionized the movie industry.
- Uber disrupted the taxi industry.
- Spotify, Pandora and Apple transformed the music industry.
- The iPhone changed the camera industry.
- Amazon changed shopping.
- Tesla disrupted the automobile business.
- Zelle changed how payments are made.

These changes illustrate creative destruction. Something is destroyed but something is also created. This is how progress in our free-market economy works.

It is often easier to notice the destruction than to appreciate the creation. When a company goes out of business, it makes the news. When a company lays off a lot of workers, it also makes the news. But when four friends get together to start a new business, it rarely gets attention. It might take them years to build a successful business that actually gets noticed. We see the destruction immediately but miss the creation.

Creative destruction is about dynamism and

innovation. What drives this disruption is the endless pursuit of sales and profits. Companies can only achieve lasting profits by serving customers better than competitors—with better products, lower prices, higher quality or superior customer service.

THE REALITY OF FAILURE

Risk-taking and failure go hand in hand. Creating and building a business involves significant uncertainty. Most startups fail and entrepreneurs know it.

Rarely does an entrepreneur get it right the first time. Every successful entrepreneur has a story of failures and false starts. It takes many iterations of trial and error to build something that works. Failure is a natural part of entrepreneurship.

As I mentioned earlier, only half of all small businesses survive longer than five years and just one in three make it past ten years[7]. Starting a business and achieving success is a tough road.

Venture capital firms invest capital in thousands of companies every year, most of which fail. These venture capital firms are managed by some of the smartest investors and most successful entrepreneurs in the U.S. If they can't figure it out, who can? No one knows for sure which startup companies will succeed.

The average entrepreneur is working on their 2.3 start-up. In other words, the first two businesses failed and now they're working on the third one. They don't get it right the first time, but they keep trying.

People learn more from failure than from success, and this is especially true for entrepreneurs. They learn hard lessons about the market, about their technology, their product and their customers' needs. Now they're smarter.

---

[7] Small Business Administration, "Survival Rates and Firm Age," https://advocacy.sba.gov/wp-content/uploads/2019/06/Startup-Rates-and-Firm-Age.pdf

They use this knowledge to do a better job when they continue building or when they start another business.

Speaking of failure, let's consider bankruptcy. One benefit of the United States' culture of risk-taking is that we allow for bankruptcy, which enables entrepreneurs to get back on their feet and start over again. This tolerance for failure is an important part of the free market process.

Failure is Frequent

It is not only small companies that fail; large established companies can fail too. You may recognize several large firms that failed: Kodak, Blockbuster Video, Sears, MCI, American Motors and Toys"R"Us.

Take Sears for example. Sears, Roebuck and Co. began in 1893 as a mail-order service that sold a wide variety of products through their catalog. Eventually they built department stores and had 1,000 stores at their peak. In 2005 they merged with Kmart and had 3,500 stores. Sears expanded its product line to include home appliances and later, Allstate insurance and the Discover credit card. It had strong brands like Kenmore, Craftsman and Diehard. The company was extremely profitable.

A failure to change eventually led to the company's downfall. Stores became dingy and fell into disrepair. The merger with Kmart cheapened the Sears brand. The firm lacked the resources to innovate or enter the age of e-commerce.

Sears faced stiff competition from Walmart, Target and Amazon. Sears' retail sales collapsed. Today Sears operates just eight stores—down from 3,500 at its peak.

DeLorean's Failure

In contrast to Tesla's success, John DeLorean's venture was a spectacular failure. The company had many positive elements: stunning design, stainless steel body and gullwing doors.

The company got off to a good start. It raised $160 million in loans, grants and guarantees from the British Government. The company raised $9 million from U.S. automobile dealers and $20 million via a research limited partnership. Several books have been written about the DeLorean Motor Company and its failure; this is the short version. (I worked at DeLorean for a brief stint in 1979.)

John Delorean may have been a good engineer, but he was not a good businessman. He made one poor decision after another, including an alleged cocaine deal.

Image: Alex Kropp from Pixabay

The reasons for failure were many, but the primary factors were bad management, costly production, inadequate financing and poor market timing. The car was also high priced and underpowered. In 2025 dollars, it cost $91,000 and had only 132 horsepower!

John DeLorean paid himself a very generous salary ($2 million) which is not smart for a startup company. In addition, there were some questionable financial arrangements at the company in which money flowed to DeLorean's personal accounts.

In my view, the company could have succeeded with competent management and proper financing. There was clearly a sufficient market for an innovative and unique car.

Tupperware's Failure

Tupperware is a well-known food storage brand founded in 1946 by Earl Tupper. It has been a household name for 79 years. The stock was listed on the New York Stock Exchange in 1996 and had sales of $1.3 billion. It was a very successful business.

Originally, Tupperware sold its products by salespeople who hosted Tupperware parties in their homes, providing drinks and snacks, demonstrating products and taking orders.

The best year was 2013 when revenue reached $2.6 billion. Then revenues began to shrink and the company's direct selling model began to flounder. Online shopping had transformed retail, and companies like Amazon made it easy for people to shop from home. Competition offered similar products both online and in stores. The company began selling products on Amazon.com and at Target in 2022, but competitors already dominated online and retail. Tupperware filed for bankruptcy in October 2024,

What is the lesson here? The company failed to adapt its sales strategy until it was too late. Being slow to change can kill a business. Tupperware had a successful model for decades, but when the market shifted, they could not adapt fast enough.

WHY DO BUSINESSES FAIL?

Businesses fail for four primary reasons:

1. Product. The product misses the mark; it is not what the market wants. It doesn't address a real need, may be overpriced or there simply is no viable market for it. People are not interested in purchasing the product.

2. Cash. The company does not have sufficient cash to continue operating. They cannot generate enough sales revenue to pay bills, may have burned through investment capital and are unable to raise additional funding.

3. Skill set. They don't have the right team. Businesses have many moving parts and need people with diverse skills. They fail because they lack the right set of talents.

4. Competition. A business might have a product that solves a real market need, but competition is just too tough. The company cannot match competitors on price, quality, delivery or customer service.

Even the biggest and best companies in the United States experience change and upheaval. The Fortune 500 ranks the largest U.S. companies by revenue. Every year about 25 companies join the list because their sales have increased. The same number of companies fall off the list.

Since 2003, 52% of the companies have disappeared from the list[8]. The reasons are many: technology

[8] Yahoo Finance, Access Newswire, https://finance.yahoo.com/news/insight-report-finds-52-companies-163000568.html

disruption, lack of innovation, increased competition, failure to adapt to changing markets, economic turmoil and poor leadership. In addition, several companies were acquired.

The relentless pace of competition, innovation and shifts in the economy are the reasons for this revolving door. This ongoing creative destruction is what drives economic growth and prosperity.

7 BEHIND THE SCENES—THE UNGLAMOROUS ASPECTS

Entrepreneurs face many challenges in building their companies. This chapter illustrates some of the more mundane operational realities that entrepreneurs encounter behind the scenes—the practical aspects that are not often visible to the public.

Managing Cash

The primary challenge for every entrepreneur is managing the company's cash flow. Keeping an eye on the money is critical. A business must have enough cash on hand to pay the bills and especially to make payroll.

Most companies do not have a steady stream of revenues so managing the cash flow can be a challenge. Where will the revenues come from next month? Will we have enough money to pay the bills? Those questions can keep entrepreneurs awake at night.

Loans and Personal Guarantees

Many businesses require some kind of financing to fill in gaps in cash flow. Sometimes a company can obtain a bank loan but the entrepreneur must personally guarantee it in most cases. That means that personal assets are at risk. If they cannot get a business loan, entrepreneurs often borrow against their house.

Hiring and Firing

Hiring and firing is a critical responsibility for entrepreneurs. Hiring is difficult. How can you know if a person will be a productive employee? The entrepreneur or manager must typically interview multiple candidates for a job opening and they may have multiple interviews with the top candidates. It is a lot of work. If an employee does not work out, it can create complications and the interview process must begin anew.

Image by 6aathif_aarifeen from Pixabay

Firing someone is even more stressful, but sometimes it must be done. The other employees always know who is not performing or not pulling their weight. Entrepreneurs lose sleep when they know they must fire someone the next day.

In addition, businesses are always at risk of being sued for wrongful termination, sexual harassment, racism, sexism etc. The business owners must deal with these issues and potential risks.

Managing Resources

Managing resources is a constant challenge. Should we buy another delivery truck? Is our office space big enough? Do we need to hire a customer service manager? What about engineering, should we add an engineer? These issues are changing constantly and the entrepreneur must prioritize the best they can to keep the company running smoothly.

A business that requires inventory has an additional set of challenges. How much inventory should they keep on hand? They don't want to buy too much inventory nor too little. What about seasonal inventory? That complicates things. Some types of inventory can spoil, for example, food at a deli. Purchasing the correct amount and timing of inventory is a constant challenge for entrepreneurs; mistakes can be costly.

Administrative Tasks

The entrepreneur must handle budgeting and bookkeeping, manage payroll and employee records, ensure compliance with regulations and prepare tax reports for city, state and federal taxes. They also manage customer accounts, software systems, insurance coverage, contracts and leases. Many of these tasks are tedious but critical; a missed deadline could mean penalties.

Image by ernestoeslava

Some companies are large enough to hire a person to handle these administrative tasks. Outside services are available for many of these tasks, but there is a cost. Bookkeepers, accountants, payroll services and virtual assistants can take on some administrative functions.

Software and software services can also automate some tasks. Despite these options, entrepreneurs must still oversee these functions and many small business owners end up handling most administrative tasks themselves, especially in the early stages.

Sales Calls and Keeping Customers Satisfied

Making sales calls is not the most fun aspect of running a business. Some entrepreneurs are good at sales calls and actually enjoy it. But others don't particularly enjoy it, nor are they good at it. But they know it must be done. That is part of the discipline of being an entrepreneur. One must hustle and bring in new customers.

Every business exists to serve its customers. Managing the customer relationship is of paramount importance. Providing good service is key for most businesses and it takes an ongoing effort.

Image by VinzentWeinbeer from Pixabay

Keeping up with competitors is another challenge that entrepreneurs face. Every company has competitors who may have better products, cheaper products, greater variety, better service...there is always something.

Growth and Strategy

As a business grows, the entrepreneur must figure out how to scale the company in the most efficient way. This is a nice problem to have since growth is always a good thing.

If the entrepreneur is building a business that needs

additional financing, raising this capital will require significant time and effort. Contacting and meeting with investors can take huge amounts of time. Attorneys must typically get involved because financing involves the sale of stock or securities.

Entrepreneurs need to have a longer-term strategy. Where is the company going? What types of products and services will it offer in the future? Many entrepreneurs do not actually have a strategic plan. They are consumed with the day-to-day problems and are just trying to keep their heads above water. Others realize that markets change and customer needs change. They must figure out how to address these challenges.

Dealing with all these challenges produces significant stress. These challenges explain why entrepreneurship is not for everyone—but those who persist create the businesses that drive our economy forward.

Entrepreneurs must also face external economic realities. Even the most determined entrepreneurs must contend with the harsh realities of competition and markets. The market does not care about passion—it only rewards results.

Part II. Market Dynamics

Markets are characterized by competition and voluntary exchange. Competition forces businesses to improve, giving us lower prices, higher quality, greater choice and higher wages. Investment powers innovation and growth. Growth creates jobs and raises living standards.

8 COMPETITION ROCKS

Competition is a wonderful thing, but there are numerous misconceptions about how it makes us better off. You hear phrases like "cutthroat competition" or "dog-eat-dog competition." Here is what really happens.

Businesses compete against other businesses for your dollars. They compete to sell their products and services to you. Restaurants compete for your dining business. Movie theaters compete for your entertainment business. Clothing stores compete to sell you the latest fashions.

Competition forces businesses to improve. If a business doesn't improve, competitors will do a better job and attract the customers. The customers decide who gets to stay in business.

There are four significant benefits of competition:

- Lower prices
- Higher quality
- Greater choice
- Higher wages

Competition Reduces Prices

Companies work hard to reduce their costs so that they can cut prices. Lower prices deliver a double benefit: increased sales and competitive advantage over rivals. The winner, of course, is the customer.

Why would a company ever lower its prices? Wouldn't that reduce its profit? Doesn't it seem more likely that companies would want to *raise* their prices? As discussed in the chapter on profits, companies would love to raise prices, but competition prevents this. If they raise prices, they will lose customers to competitors offering lower prices.

EXAMPLES OF PRICE COMPETITION

The best way to illustrate this point about the beauty of competition is with a few examples. Three cases demonstrate the point:

- Television sets
- Lasik eye surgery
- Commissions for trading stocks

Television Sets And Lasik Surgery

The drop in the price of television sets has been nothing short of miraculous. Today you can buy a 50-inch Samsung television, which is a good brand, for $250. A 65-inch model would set you back only $400. This is an amazing value for the money.

Five years ago, a comparable Panasonic television sold for $2,600. Ten years ago, a 50-inch television was priced at $6,000. Twenty years ago, a flat panel plasma TV sold for $22,900[9].

Lasik eye surgery is another great example of competition pushing prices down. Lasik eye surgery is considered a cosmetic or elective procedure; therefore, it is not covered by health insurance. It is a real market and doctors compete for the business.

Lasik surgery corrects vision for people who are nearsighted, farsighted or have astigmatism. Many people can eliminate the need for glasses entirely. The cost of Lasik has been falling for decades since its FDA approval in 1995. The cost was about $5,000 per eye in the mid-1990s[10]. The cost of Lasik surgery in 2025 was down to about $2,000 per eye. It costs even less if there is a promotion. The drop in price occurred even with significant technical breakthroughs that made the process more effective and less risky.

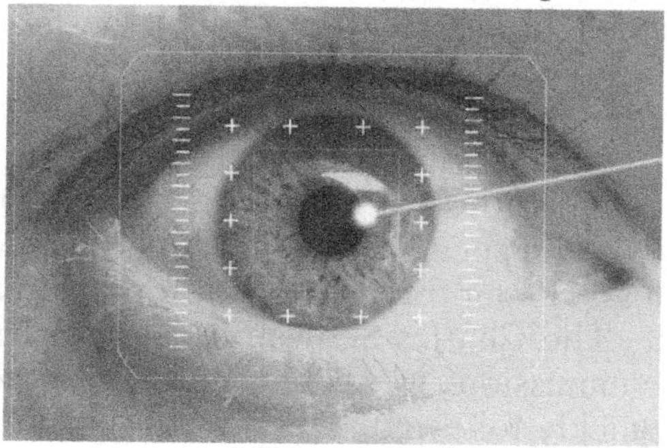

People are smart about how they spend their money and they shop around. The average Lasik customer calls four

[9] Geoffrey Morrison, "Are TVs really cheaper than ever? We go back a few decades to see," Nov. 23, 2017, CNET, https://www.cnet.com/news/are-tvs-really-cheaper-than-ever-we-go-back-a-few-decades-to-see/

[10] MarketWatch, Sean Masaki Flynn, "The U.S. can Slash Health-Care Costs," Nov. 9, 2019, https://www.marketwatch.com/story/the-us-can-slash-health-care-costs-75-with-2-fundamental-changes-and-without-medicare-for-all-2019-08-15

different doctors to compare prices. Lasik surgery is an excellent example of competition reducing prices.

Trading Commissions are Free

The cost to buy or sell shares of stock is now zero dollars. That's right, zero. If you purchase stock, no matter how many shares, the commission is zero. If you bought 10 shares of Tesla stock for $3,000, the commission you pay is zero. How is this possible?

The answer is competition. Discount stock brokers compete for customers by lowering their prices for trading stocks. They make money in other ways—by earning interest on cash balances and by lending on margin.

To buy or sell a stock in 1962, you would have paid almost 1% of the transaction amount as a commission. This changed in 1975 when regulators abolished fixed-rate trading commissions. Entrepreneurs started discount stock brokerage firms which began the move toward lower commissions. In the late 1980s, the average commission was $45.

Competition among these brokerage firms reduced commissions to $30 in 2015. For people trading online (without speaking to a broker), the commission was even less, $15 per trade. Then it dropped to $7 and then to $5.

The Charles Schwab brokerage firm reduced trading commissions to zero in 2019. The other brokerage firms quickly followed. The price has dropped from 1% of the transaction amount to zero. That truly is amazing. Thanks to competition, stock trades are now commission-free.

MORE CHOICES AND BETTER QUALITY

Greater competition means more companies are selling products and services. The result is a larger selection. Having more choices is an excellent aspect of our free market system.

Video streaming is a market sector with a multitude of

choices. In the beginning, there was only Netflix. Now the list is long and getting longer: Amazon Prime Video, Disney+, Hulu, HBO Max, Paramount+, Peacock, AppleTV+, ESPN+ and YouTube TV. Several new services have entered the market, some you may not have heard of: Tubi, Starz, Crackle, Vudu, SlingTV, Kanopy, FuboTV, KweliTV, Plex, Crunchyroll and Twitch. People have a cornucopia of choices for entertainment. These companies are all competing for your entertainment dollars.

Image b JillWellington from Pixabay

Increasing the quality of their products is another way that businesses attract customers. One way to improve quality is to make products smarter. Everything seems to be getting smart these days. My refrigerator beeps at me when I leave the door open. My car tells me when a tire is low on air. It even tells me which tire.

The spackle that I use to patch my wall changes color from pink to white when it has dried long enough to sand or paint. Smart spackle! The business that produces this spackle was also smart because now its product performs better than competitors'.

Competition Increases Wages

Why do wages go up? Why don't they just stay the same? The answer is that businesses must compete for employees. To get the best employees, a business must pay someone more than a competitor does.

Ponder this question: Why does anyone make *more* than the minimum wage? Some high-tech engineers make

$225,000, that is seven times more than a minimum wage worker's $30,000. Why? A good sales manager might make $200,000. Why do they make more than the minimum $30,000? The answer is because businesses bid against each other for these professionals, driving wages up.

Over the years I have had fun asking people a variation of that question. I ask them why *they* make more than the minimum wage. They are a bit flummoxed with the question. At first, they are insulted, as if I am suggesting they are not capable or valuable. But once we get past that they are still baffled.

"Why do you make more than the minimum wage," I continue. People stumble to answer. They say things like "I have many years of experience" or "I have a Master's degree." To which I respond—So what? Why does that translate into dollars? I continue my relentless questions until eventually they blurt out something like "Well, if they don't pay me enough, then I will go work for someone else." Exactly! And what do we call that? We call that competition. Phew!

Competition brings out the best in us. It does so in sports and it does so in life and in business. It gives us lower prices, better quality, more choices and it increases our wages. Competition makes us better off.

COOPERATION

Another market dynamic is cooperation. Businesses often cooperate with each other through vendor relationships, partnerships and alliances. These arrangements are an important part of our economy. A good example of cooperation is the connection between a manufacturing company and its parts suppliers. An auto parts company will sell parts to an auto manufacturer. This is a mutually beneficial partnership for both firms; they depend on each other for their success.

Image by Pineapple22 from Pixabay

These businesses develop trust. The auto manufacturer trusts that parts will meet quality standards, arrive on time and that problems can be resolved quickly. It is a symbiotic relationship.

Barnes & Noble and Starbucks have an alliance or licensing agreement in which Barnes & Noble operates coffee shops in its bookstores and sells Starbucks coffee drinks. This cooperation benefits customers.

Amazon cooperates with Staples and Kohl's to make returns easier for its customers. Many, but not all, products purchased on Amazon.com may be returned to a Kohl's store or a Staples store. This saves customers the hassle of packing and shipping items back to Amazon. It also increases the foot traffic at the retail stores. It is a good complementary relationship.

Bogus Analogies

When considering business and competition, it is important to avoid bogus metaphors and analogies. These misleading comparisons promote incorrect reasoning and disguise how competition and markets actually work.

You hear a lot about business being a jungle. "It's a jungle out there." We have heard that phrase for years. Have you ever been to a jungle? In a jungle, animals actually *do* eat each other. I have not been to a jungle, but I have seen it on television. It isn't pretty.

Business is not a jungle, not even close. Business is about cooperation. It is a win for the customer and a win for the business. They cooperate and both are better off. The lion does not negotiate with the giraffe. The hyenas do not make a deal with the zebras or gazelles. No cooperating there.

Another analogy that you hear refers to "dog-eat-dog competition." Do dogs really eat dogs? Have you ever seen a dog eat another dog? I didn't think so. That is a bad analogy. If business was truly that way, you might see the headline: "Jeff Bezos has Bill Gates for dinner." You can ponder that one.

9 WHAT MARKETS ACTUALLY DO

A market is simply people connecting to trade—nothing more, nothing less. Markets expand everyone's options. Instead of being limited to what you can produce yourself, you can access the products and services of millions of other people. Markets are human nature in action. You participate in markets every day without thinking about it because trading with others is what humans naturally do.

A market is a process, not a place. Whether you're at Home Depot or shopping on eBay, you're participating in the same fundamental process—people connecting to trade. The location doesn't matter. What matters is that buyers and sellers can find each other and make deals.

Markets don't need a central location to function. The housing market proves this—there's no "house store," yet millions of homes change hands every year. Buyers and sellers find each other through agents, websites and word of mouth. The market exists in the connections between people, not in any building.

Some markets are local, others global. You buy a house locally but can buy baseball cards from anywhere in the country. Geography matters less than the ability of buyers and sellers to connect.

Yet markets are widely misunderstood. Critics paint them as chaotic and dangerous, requiring heavy regulation to protect people. Others think free markets mean no rules at all. Many believe markets routinely "fail" and need government intervention. These misconceptions miss how markets actually function.

Markets are Voluntary

The most important thing to understand about markets is that participation is always voluntary. No one forces you to buy the apples, the Jeep or the house. No one forces the sellers to sell either. Every transaction happens because both sides believe they will benefit.

Markets are interactions between producers who each bring value to the exchange. This means every market participant is also a producer. You can only buy things consistently if you produce something of value first—whether that's goods, services or labor.

Prices are Information

Prices are information systems. Every price tells you what people truly value, not what they say they value. There are no right or wrong prices—only prices that reflect what buyers and sellers actually agree to pay.

People are shrewd about how they spend their money. They shop around, compare prices, hunt for sales. This is smart economic calculation on their part.

Businesses use price information to make production decisions. If raw materials cost too much or the finished product sells for too little, they won't manufacture a product. Prices naturally guide resources to where they're most valued.

When gas prices spike, that is the market telling you gasoline is scarce relative to demand. The high price encourages conservation and signals producers to increase supply.

Markets Do Not Fail

The idea that markets can fail misunderstands what markets fundamentally are. Markets cannot fail because markets don't promise anything. When critics say "markets don't provide this or that," they fundamentally mistake what markets are. The role of a market is simply to connect buyers and sellers so people can provide for themselves.

If you price your bike for sale at $700 on Facebook Marketplace and no one buys it, did the market fail? Of course not. The market is telling you something: your price is wrong. Adjust the price and the bike will sell.

Image by alain-frechette from Pixabay

Consider the 2008 housing crash. Prices soared for years, then collapsed dramatically. Many buyers put down zero money and it was ridiculously easy to buy houses. Anyone could flip houses and make a quick gain. How could this continue? Of course, it could not. The market crashed. Many called this "market failure," but that gets it backwards. Rising prices were the market working when demand exceeded supply. Falling prices were also the market working—prices had gotten too high. Markets simply reflect what buyers and sellers decide.

What do you do when no one wants to buy your house? The answer is simple. You lower the price. At some point the house will be affordable to a buyer and it will sell. It is all about price. Housing prices go up and housing prices go down. That's what markets do. You may not like the prices, but that does not mean that the market failed. Markets just are.

Markets are morally neutral. They do not have feelings or opinions. Markets do not have a conscience. These are human traits. Markets just process information and coordinate voluntary exchanges. When people don't like the results, they blame the market instead of recognizing that markets simply reflect human choices.

Image by Pavel Danilyuk from Pixabay

Markets reward businesses that serve customers better than their competitors. But serving customers better requires constant improvement and innovation—and that requires investment. The next chapter explains why investment is critical for progress and, interestingly, how the rich recycle their money.

10 INVESTMENT: THE ENGINE OF PROGRESS

How Capital Drives Innovation

Investment fuels all growth. Entrepreneurs need money to start their companies and to build their companies. This funding helps these businesses get off the ground and flourish. Investment is how our country makes progress and raises our standard of living.

There are many misunderstandings about investment. People do not realize:

- Investment is critically important.
- Almost every startup needs capital.
- Businesses need capital to grow.
- Investment comes from savings.

Investment means putting up some cash to pay for the things that a business needs to expand or to develop new products. This money is used to hire employees, rent an office, buy equipment, buy raw materials and other business essentials.

When a business purchases a new delivery truck, that is investment. When the yard maintenance guy saves his money and buys a new lawnmower, that is investment. When a pizza restaurant buys a new pizza oven, that is investment. When a large company raises capital to build a new factory, that is investment. When three young women start a new business and raise money from investors, that too is investment.

Today we have all kinds of wonderful technology—streaming video, smart phones, GPS, Fitbits and more. Every one of these magical things was made possible because of investment. Without investment, they would not exist.

Image by Tama66 from Pixabay

Capital to Start Up

Every entrepreneur needs capital to start their business. An entrepreneur cannot grow their company with effort alone. It costs money to rent office space, buy computers, pay salaries, etc. Even if an entrepreneur works out of their home, they still need money or savings to pay their personal bills until the business can produce some sales.

There are plenty of entrepreneurs with ideas—but without capital their dreams will remain unfulfilled. Some businesses require only a small amount of capital to get going; others require substantial capital, but every business requires some capital to get off the ground.

Small businesses are almost always short of money. The primary reason is timing. The owner must build out the pizza store, buy a pizza oven, and hire and train employees long before the first slice of Kristen and Travis' special pepperoni pizza is sold. It's all about cash flow.

Cash comes in and cash goes out. But the cash does not come in until the pizza store has already been built. So, Kristen and Travis need investment.

Capital to Grow

If Kristen and Travis want to open that second pizza restaurant across town, they must have saved up enough money or get a loan or investment, perhaps from uncle Giovanni.

If a company wants to build a new factory that will cost $100 million, they will need to raise capital. They rarely have this much cash on hand, so they will have to get bank loans or sell bonds or shares of stock.

Image by analogicus from Pixabay

Most businesses do not earn enough profits to finance their own growth. Companies almost always require outside capital to expand because growth requires large upfront investments—developing new products, building facilities, hiring staff—before those investments generate any revenue.

Investing in the iPad

Apple's development of the iPad illustrates how investment comes first. Before the iPad came on the market, Apple had to hire designers, engineers, marketing people, salespeople and so on. Paying the salaries of these employees required the investment of a significant amount of capital.

Where did Apple get the cash to pay these people before any iPads were sold? Apple had been a successful company for many years and it had generated significant profits and cash. If Apple had been a young startup company with the idea for the iPad, it would have to raise money from investors before it could develop the product. In its startup days, Apple *did* raise investment capital from the Rockefeller family. Investment is the first step in the chain of events that leads to a product being invented, produced and sold to customers.

SAVING MUST HAPPEN FIRST

Savings make all investment possible. If a person wants to make an investment, they must first earn and save the money. They choose not to spend the money, but to save it.

People can do three things with their money:

- Spend it
- Invest it
- Give it away

There are no other choices. This is true whether a person is poor, middle-class or wealthy.

Saving requires some degree of deferred gratification. Seed corn is a good example of how saving works. If you eat all your corn, you will have no seeds to plant for next year's crop. The smart farmer saves some seed corn to plant next year.

Image by maitree rimthong from Pixabay

A business, no matter how large or small, must save money to purchase the productive tools and equipment that it needs to expand its business. A carpenter who needs a new table saw must save money before he can purchase the saw. A teenager who wants to buy a car must work and save money until they have enough cash to purchase the car.

Everyone talks about spending driving the economy, but investment is what really makes things happen. Companies invest to produce products before people can buy the products. Without investment, companies cannot grow or even get started.

Is Saving Bad?

Since many believe that spending drives the economy, then spending must be good. If spending is good, then saving must be bad—after all, money that you save is money that you don't spend.

Wait a minute. Saving is bad? What if I am saving money to buy a car? or saving for college? or saving to buy a house? or saving for retirement? Are these things bad for the economy? Well, obviously not. How could saving possibly be bad?

Saving is essential because saving is where investment comes from. Investment is the critical first step in creating jobs, new innovations, new products, new drugs or new technologies. Investment makes those things happen and investment comes from money that has been saved. It all starts with savings.

Robinson Crusoe's money printing adventures in Chapter 14 illustrate this spending concept in an entertaining way.

THE RICH RECYCLE THEIR MONEY

Investors have money to invest because they have saved money. People who are well off don't have to spend all their money to live; therefore, they have money left over to save and therefore, to invest.

If a wealthy person deposits some money into a bank, the bank will lend that money to businesses. If an individual buys some shares of stock in the stock market, someone else is selling those shares. The seller then has cash to invest elsewhere, purchase a different stock or spend it on something—perhaps a bathroom remodel or their children's tuition. The point is that the money is spent; it does not just sit there.

Some people think that wealthy people do not invest their money productively—that they "put it under the mattress" or just keep the cash in the bank where it does no good. This could not be further from the truth. Wealthy people are generally smart about how they handle their investments and they often have professional advisers to help them.

Image by rotekirsche20 from Pixabay

Wealthy investors spread their money across many productive uses—a portfolio of stocks and bonds, real estate and other assets. They may invest in a startup company or an apartment building. This investment capital flows directly into productive assets that are critical for economic growth.

A remarkable example of how the rich recycle their money is PayPal. You probably know PayPal; it facilitates payments on the Internet (and it owns Venmo). It was founded in 1998 by Peter Thiel and Max Levchin. They sold PayPal to eBay in 2002 for $1.5 billion. They used the gains from their PayPal stock to invest in other startups. The investors, founders and employees of PayPal have come to be known as the "PayPal Mafia." Many of these investments became extremely successful companies;

Image by brettjordan from Pixabay

you may recognize some names—Palantir Technologies, Square, LinkedIn, Tesla, SpaceX, Yelp, YouTube, Slide, Yammer and Kiva. Truly amazing! These investors and tech entrepreneurs recycled their money in a very productive way that created new companies, new jobs, new technologies and amazing new products.

Where Does Money Come from to Start Companies?

Startup capital typically comes from the entrepreneur's personal savings or from a loan secured by the equity in their home. The entrepreneur's family and friends might provide funding as well.

Beyond personal resources, individual investors become important. These investors include doctors, lawyers and other professionals who earn a good living and have money to invest. These are called angel investors.

Successful entrepreneurs, like the PayPal guys, are an important source of startup capital as well. They may have sold their company and have capital to invest. They enjoy the entrepreneurial process and want to be involved with interesting startup companies.

When larger amounts are needed, say more than a few million dollars, the funds typically come from professional venture capital firms.

Businesses Invest Continually

Most companies continually invest in the growth of their businesses. A company might start a new product line, build a new factory, purchase new machinery or open a branch office in Denver.

Investment enables the company to hire people to work in the new factory, work on the new product line, or work in the new office in Denver. Investment creates jobs.

The United States has very sophisticated capital markets. These markets enable businesses to raise capital to invest in new projects. We have a stock market that is generally trusted, free from corruption and it provides liquidity, so people can easily and inexpensively buy and sell stocks. Access to capital is an area where the United States excels compared to the rest of the world.

The U.S. capital markets enable companies to obtain financing to expand, create jobs and provide us with remarkable products and services. Investment is the foundation for our high standard of living. (Appendix C explains how Wall Street benefits us.)

The next topic—growth—is widely misunderstood. Why is growth important? What exactly is growth anyway?

11 THE POWER OF GROWTH

Growth is critical for improving our standard of living. Growth alleviates human misery; it makes our lives longer, healthier and better.

There are numerous misconceptions about growth. Why do we need to grow? Why do we need more stuff? Doesn't it just use up our precious resources? Does growth really help the poor? How does it make us better off?

The short answer to these questions is that growth raises the living standards for all Americans. Growth means that more jobs are being created and that people earn higher incomes. It means that innovative new products and services are being invented. Growth means new drugs and healthcare solutions are being discovered.

In this chapter, I will use the term growth in the broad sense. Growth means progress and innovation—it does not just mean producing more stuff. Innovation plays an important role in improving our standard of living. The second half of the chapter explores innovation.

Good Things Happen

When our economy grows:

- More jobs are created
- People have more disposable income
- Businesses thrive
- The stock market goes up
- Retirement savings grow
- Charitable giving increases

As our economy grows, more jobs will be needed. Where will the jobs come from? New jobs are created by companies that are expanding. If a company is not growing, it does not create new jobs.

Growth is important for almost every business. A company that doesn't grow in an expanding economy is actually losing market share. This means that other companies are providing goods or services that customers prefer. Growth also increases tax revenues, which helps government finances.

Understanding Growth

Growth is an economy's ability to satisfy the wants and needs of people. There is no right answer about what these wants and needs should be. They are whatever people desire. They may include a new e-bike, a new frying pan, a larger house, healthier food or a better way to treat disease. Satisfying these wants increases people's well-being. Growth means that companies are creating and producing new products and services and attracting new customers. It means that revenues are increasing and jobs are being created. Wages go up as companies compete for workers.

Examples of growth include things like Apple coming out with a new iPhone. The opening of new stores, such as Trader Joe's or IKEA, makes products and conveniences available to more people. A new Walmart store brings lower prices, more products and new jobs to poorer neighborhoods. Growth includes things like a new apartment building being constructed or a yard maintenance company adding a tree-trimming service to attract customers.

New technologies and inventions generate growth. We play music using Spotify or Pandora rather than purchasing compact discs, cassettes or vinyl records. These new music technologies are growth. Growth includes new methods to publish books such as Kindle Direct Publishing. The progress that we are experiencing is truly remarkable.

Image by Andrea Piacquadio from Pexels

Growth is generally measured by the increase in gross domestic product, or GDP. This measures our total output of goods and services. Since the early 1800s, GDP growth has averaged 1.9% per year in the U.S. During bad years growth can be zero. In a recession, growth is negative, meaning the economy shrinks. In boom times, growth can be 3% or 4%. In an economy as large as the United States, 3% growth is a *huge* increase in the production of goods and services.

Taking it for Granted

Americans tend to take growth for granted. We have experienced growth for so many years over our lives that it seems like the normal state. New technologies are constantly being developed that make our lives easier and more interesting—new movies, new games, new services, new electric cars and other innovative products.

It has not always been this way. If you look at human history, growth did not occur on a steady basis. There were spurts of growth at different points in time, but it was never ongoing and constant. History shows that growth is not a given; we should not take it for granted.

Why Must a Business Grow?

It is important for most businesses to grow. A growing company can experiment with new ideas. It can be creative in finding new ways to serve customers and attract new types of customers, making business interesting and gratifying. When a business is growing, it gives its employees the opportunity to develop and flourish. Employees learn new skills and get promoted. They take on new challenges, making the work rewarding for them.

Not every business needs to grow. Consider a family business, such as a hardware store or a restaurant, that is thriving nicely. They serve the same clientele year after year; revenues are steady, and the business is profitable enough for the employees and owners to make a living. They are happy with their situation and growth is not an objective for them.

Growth Means More Jobs and Higher Pay

Entrepreneurs are continually evaluating their businesses to decide whether they should expand or not—should they bring out a new product line? Should they hire more people? Entrepreneurs are always pondering ways to improve their businesses, and this growth creates jobs.

As businesses grow, they compete with other firms to hire the best employees. This competition raises wages and salaries. More people rise into the middle class.

Businesses and markets are dynamic. As firms expand and contract, jobs are created and destroyed. Every day, about 80,000 jobs[11] are destroyed in the U.S., but a slightly *greater* number of jobs are created every day. Things are always changing. A healthy turnover in the economy is good; new firms innovate and push out the less productive firms.

Growth Helps the Poor

Helping the poor is probably the most significant consequence of growth. The reason is not always obvious to critics of growth, but it is crucial to understand.

When the economy grows, people with fewer skills—often poor people—who could not find work can now get jobs because businesses need more workers. More jobs are available for those with limited skills. In addition, many part-time workers can become full-time workers.

A growing economy produces more goods and services. When more goods are produced, supply increases and prices go down. As a result, goods are more affordable for people with limited incomes.

Economic growth is especially important in developing countries where there is more poverty. Growth increases their standard of living dramatically. The primary driver for reducing poverty is not government transfer programs; it is economic growth.

South Korea's Transformation

South Korea provides a powerful example of how economic growth transforms living standards. In the early 1960s, South Korea was a very poor country with per capita income similar to many African nations.

The country focused on education, investment and entrepreneurship and achieved growth averaging over 7%

---

[11] Federal Reserve Bank of St. Louis, "Fewer Jobs Are Being Created and Being Destroyed," 4/2/2015, www.stlouisfed.org/on-the-economy/2015/april/fewer-jobs-are-being-created-and-being-destroyed

per year for decades. Today, South Korea is a high-income country with world-class industries in electronics, automobiles and entertainment. This transformation occurred within a single generation, lifting millions from poverty to prosperity. Singapore achieved similar success, evolving from a resource-poor island nation to one of the world's wealthiest countries.

Growth is not just an economic statistic—it represents real improvements in people's lives, from better healthcare and education to expanded opportunities and reduced poverty.

The Opposite of Growth

We have been discussing the good things that happen when a business is growing. What about the opposite? Let's consider a company that is *not* growing. What are the effects of not growing?

The opposite of growth is stagnation and decline. If a business is not growing, it is certainly not creating any new jobs. It may lay off employees or ask some to take a salary cut. It surely will not be giving people raises.

A company that is not growing is unlikely to develop new products and will probably lose ground to competition. A stagnant business also limits the potential of its employees. Talented workers may quit to find better opportunities for career advancement elsewhere.

Some small businesses may not wish to grow—like our family restaurant example. They may be perfectly content with the way things are. That is okay but it does limit the potential for advancement for the employees.

The game of Monopoly illustrates a "no growth" economy; it is a miniature economy where players buy and sell properties and collect rents. But Monopoly is static with no innovation. No new types of hotels are invented. No Airbnb emerges to disrupt the market. In the real world, Airbnb turned the hotel industry upside down and Uber transformed the taxi industry.

Do not assume that the real economy is a bigger version of the game of Monopoly. It is not an accurate representation of our economy. There is no growth or innovation. The real economy is a growing and everchanging ecosystem.

Critics often worry that growth harms the environment. However, innovation has been our best way to solve environmental problems. Today's solar panels generate more energy with less material than those from a decade ago. Modern manufacturing has become more efficient. New buildings use less energy per square foot and electric vehicles are beginning to replace combustion engines.

Growth often means using resources smarter, not just using more of them. When countries get richer, they usually spend more money on protecting the environment. Growth and protecting the environment can work together.

INNOVATION IS VITAL

Innovation and advances in technology are the driving forces behind economic growth. They are the primary drivers of job growth in the United States.

Image by WikiImages

Americans tend to take innovation for granted. After all, we have been experiencing remarkable innovation all our lives, no matter how old we are.

Basic research is important, but it does not fuel most innovation. Innovation occurs because of the obsession and tinkering of engineers, inventors and entrepreneurs who are trying to solve specific technical, business or customer problems.

Entrepreneurs are the heart of the economy and their innovations are essential for progress. They start the companies and they take the risks; there is no growth without risk-taking. Innovation also makes some companies obsolete and they end up going out of business. The invention of wireless technologies, for example, has made traditional landline telephones obsolete.

Innovation is especially important to improve the standard of living of poor people. As new products are invented and improved, prices come down. New technologies and manufacturing improvements mean that flat screen TVs are now affordable by people with low incomes. That is good.

Image by StockSnap

Our economy has changed over time from one based on agriculture to one based on manufacturing to one now dominated by services. In the year 1800, about three quarters of the U.S. labor force worked in agriculture. Today, it is less than 3% and we produce much more food. At the end of World War II, manufacturing employed one third of the workforce. Today, manufacturers employ only one tenth of our workforce. These are dramatic changes. Services are becoming an increasingly important sector of our economy. As our economy becomes more sophisticated, the service sector plays a larger role.

Progress Improves Our Lives

Growth is important, but progress is the critical element. Progress makes our lives better. America's stunning improvements in growth and progress mean that our families live richer and fuller lives.

The average income in the United States is greater than almost every other country. Middle-class income in the U.S. is substantially higher than middle-class income in Europe[12]. The average American family earns $1.00 for every $0.75 earned by the French, Italians and Germans[13]. What creates these high incomes? The key to innovation and progress is investment and economic freedom.

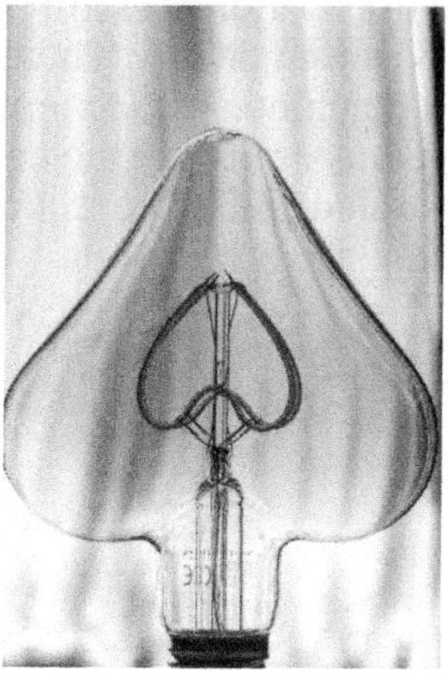
Image by Rocco Stoppoloni from Pixabay

Economic growth and freedom reinforce each other in a powerful virtuous cycle. Free societies provide the foundation for entrepreneurs to start businesses with minimal restrictions, driving innovation and economic expansion. As we have seen in countries like South Korea, growth transforms societies, lifting millions from poverty

---

[12] Bloomberg CityLab,Feargus O'Sullivan, "How America's Middle Class Compares to Europe's," Apr. 26, 2017, https://www.bloomberg.com/news/articles/2017-04-26/how-the-u-s-and-european-middle-classes-compare

[13] Pew Research Center, Fact Tank, Rakesh Kochhar, "Through an American lens, Western Europe's middle classes appear smaller," June 5, 2017, https://www.pewresearch.org/fact-tank/2017/06/05/through-an-american-lens-western-europes-middle-classes-appear-smaller/

to prosperity.

When economies grow through entrepreneurship and innovation, they create jobs, raise incomes and make products more affordable—especially helping the poor.

Part 3 addresses three common myths about how the economy works. The first myth: That the economy is like a machine. For example, if it slows down, it "needs to be jumpstarted," or the economy overheats and "needs to be cooled off." The economy is not like a machine. Let's explore the reasons.

PART III. Myths and Misconceptions

Three persistent myths distort how people think about markets and the economy. The economy is not a machine; it is not a zero-sum game with only so much to go around; and money does not make the economy go.

12 MYTH OF THE MACHINE

Many people think that our economy is like a machine or an engine. In the press, we see analogy after analogy that equate our economy with a machine. You have often heard these phrases: "We need to jump-start the economy," or we need to "prime the pump," or "The economy is overheating." There are many more.

The economy of the United States is a living organism. The economy is *not* a machine. It is an ecosystem. It is not like an engine. These ideas are nonsense.

Why is it Not Like a Machine?

First of all, what is a machine? A machine is a system in which the parts operate together to accomplish the machine's purpose. A machine is built to perform a specific task.

Many things in our lives are machines: your car, your dishwasher, even your watch. The engine in your car turns the transmission which turns the wheels which help you get to the grocery store or to the baseball game.

The parts of the machine operate the same way every time. If something breaks, such as the water pump in your car, your mechanic will install a new water pump. The new pump works exactly like the old pump. In other words, the parts are the identical and they are replaceable.

A machine is designed by someone. It is comprised of parts and gears and things that make it work. The machine works the same way every time, or at least hopefully.

An Economy is Different

An economy is very different from a machine. Yes, an economy has moving parts, but the similarity ends there. When you hop in your car and turn the key, the engine starts every time. When you press the gas pedal, the car accelerates predictably. The machine responds consistently to the same inputs.

An economy does not work the same way every time. For example, lower interest rates might spur growth in one situation and create a bubble in another. Machines are predictable; economies are not.

Most importantly, no one designed the economy. It just emerged. Machines are precisely designed and highly organized. Economies are spontaneous, constantly shifting and evolving.

THE ECONOMY IS AN ECOSYSTEM

An ecosystem is a community of organisms that interact and feed off each other. Energy and resources flow through the system naturally.

Similarly, a business ecosystem is a network of people and companies interacting with each other. They create products and services, trade, collaborate and share information. No one orchestrates this—it happens because everyone benefits.

Entrepreneurs drive ecosystem growth by starting companies and inventing new ways of doing things. Ecosystems are dynamic, constantly changing and evolving. When a company fails in the business ecosystem, other firms and investors buy their assets and use them to build and grow new companies.

Image by croisyfrom Pixabay

An ecosystem is not built on purpose; it just evolves and grows. No one planned the Brazilian rainforest, yet it thrives through countless interactions. Machines don't evolve—ecosystems do.

A Machine Does Not Grow

Our economy is obviously growing. There are more houses, cars, computers and smartphones than ever before. We produce more food, energy and new kinds of services every year.

How do we measure this growth? We measure it by GDP or gross domestic product—the sum of all goods and services that our country produces. Thirty years ago, our gross domestic product (GDP) was $9 trillion. In 2005 our GDP was $15 trillion. Ten years later we produced $18 trillion of goods and services. GDP was $29 trillion in 2024[14]. Our economy has definitely been growing.

Machines do not grow. They perform their tasks for years, but they never reproduce or evolve.

One cannot "prime the pump" as many people assert. When the government passed the stimulus bill to help the economy, almost everyone uttered phrases like "jump-start" and "prime the pump." That is not how it works. A primed pump does not start the economy.

Entrepreneurs drive the economy. Companies create the products and services that expand our economy. Our economy is not a machine waiting to be fixed. It is a dynamic, evolving ecosystem.

---

[14] https://fred.stlouisfed.org/series/GDP/

13 THE MYTH OF PIE

It is not Zero-Sum

Many people believe that our economy is a fixed pie in which one person's gain must be another's loss. This zero-sum thinking is completely wrong and economically destructive.

A fixed pie means there is only so much to go around. If one person gets more, someone else must get less. The total stays the same—wealth just changes hands. This zero-sum mindset seems logical, but it ignores how wealth actually gets created in a market economy.

Success is Not at Another's Expense

The essential point about this myth is that one person's economic success does *not* come at the expense of others.

Once I attended a small dinner party in Sun Valley, Idaho. One of the guests was a teacher at a private high school. Let's call him Peter. He was obviously an intelligent person. The conversation shifted to one of his childhood friends who had become a successful entrepreneur. The friend had started and built a business that was doing extremely well.

Peter contended that the entrepreneur should stop doing his business once he achieved a net worth of $10 million. He stated that the entrepreneur did not *need* any more money than that. "That was enough," Peter asserted. I was stunned by this statement. I pointed out that the entrepreneur was creating jobs and producing products that his customers wanted. Creating jobs and pleasing customers are two excellent outcomes. Why would you want to stop that?

Peter believed that the entrepreneur was actually taking money or assets from the rest of us. The more value the entrepreneur created, the less wealth remained for everyone else. It was obvious from his comments that he viewed business as a fixed pie or a zero-sum activity.

Peter had it exactly backwards. His entrepreneur friend was creating value, not taking it. That is why his net worth was increasing. If we stopped entrepreneurs from continuing to build their companies after they have achieved a certain milestone, say $10 million, then our country would not grow or improve very much.

Image by Artyom from Pixabay

What if Steve Jobs closed down Apple after he had achieved a $10 million net worth? Apple employed about 100 people when Jobs was worth $10 million. Apple currently employs 164,000 people, so under the scenario of stopping entrepreneurs after they have achieved $10 million in net worth, Apple would not have created the additional 163,900 jobs. Where would those people be working now? People love working at Apple. They have interesting, creative and well-paying jobs. Those 163,900 jobs exist because nobody told Steve Jobs to stop at $10 million.

The Economy is *Positive-Sum*

A positive-sum activity is one in which both parties are better off. They both win. When you buy a battery-operated leaf blower to clear your deck of pine needles and leaves, you come out ahead because it's faster and easier than sweeping or raking.

The manufacturer prefers your $160 to having another leaf blower in inventory. It doesn't cost them $160 to make the leaf blower. If it did, they wouldn't sell it at that price because there would be no profit. You valued the convenience more than your $160, or you wouldn't have bought it. After the trade, both parties are better off. It was win-win. That is a positive-sum activity.

The Rich are Getting Richer?

Along these same lines, it is important to realize that rich people do not get rich by taking from the poor. You have heard the phrase, 'the rich are getting richer and the poor getting poorer.' But even if this were true, the rich still don't get rich by taking from the poor. They get rich by creating value that didn't exist before. Wealth creation expands the total pie rather than redistributing existing slices.

An entrepreneur gets rich by creating products and services that his customers value. Creating value doesn't make poor people worse off. In fact, creating value makes the poor people better off. Let's think about cell phones for a minute. In the early days of cellular phones, a poor person could not possibly afford one of those things. They were quite expensive. (The Motorola Dyna TAC 8000X weighed almost two pounds and cost $3,995 in 1984! That's $12,100 in today's dollars.) Because of new technologies, competition and value creation, the price of cell phones has dropped dramatically. Today, people with modest incomes carry smartphones that are more powerful than room-sized computer systems in 1984.

There are 5.8 billion smart phone subscribers worldwide today[15]. The number grows every year and 71% of the world population own smart phones. Millions of new phones are designed and produced every year. We are not fighting over a fixed number of phones. If our world was a fixed pie, there would be no progress for human beings.

The rest of the economy is just like the telephone market. There are more houses, more television sets, more cars, more of everything. As the economy grows, the pie gets bigger, costs go down, prices go down and more people can afford things and we are all better off.

The zero-sum myth is not the only misconception that clouds economic thinking. Another persistent myth is the myth of money. Many believe that money drives the economy, when in reality...

---

[15] GSMA, The Mobile Economy 2025. www.gsma.com/solutions-and-impact/connectivity-for-good/mobile-economy/

14 THE MYTH OF MONEY

Robinson Crusoe and the $100 Bills!

Money doesn't make the economy go. Producing goods and services makes the economy go. Money just makes trading easier.

Those who believe that demand drives the economy think that the way to fix a struggling economy is for the government to spend money, print money and give money to people. The logic is seductive and completely wrong. You can't create prosperity by printing money. Markets are their own thing and the government cannot "fix" them. Printing, spending and giving away money does not boost the economy.

The economy is not a

machine you can jumpstart with cash. It's driven by entrepreneurs and businesses producing things that people need. Let's illustrate this point with a visit to Robinson Crusoe on his island. This story shows how people live, produce and thrive.

One day Robinson Crusoe discovered a printing press in an old shack on the island that could print perfect $100 bills. He printed money for himself and Friday, then for new castaways as they arrived. Eventually 200 people lived on the island, all with plenty of cash.

Image from Freepix

To survive, each castaway had to learn survival skills: knock down coconuts, catch fish, make a straw hat, build a lean-to, etc. Eventually they used the printed money to trade with each other instead of bartering—fish for berries or tools for food.

Whether the island had a population of 2 or 200 or even 2,000, the economic situation is precisely the same. The islanders had to produce the items they needed to survive.

Disaster!

Then one day disaster struck. A tropical storm came through and smashed many of the canoes and rafts. It decimated the farmland where they were growing crops. The storm blew over many of the lean-tos and destroyed much of their infrastructure. After the storm passed, the castaways scrambled to put things back together.

Robinson thought he had the solution. He went to his secret printing shack and printed up more $100 bills. He gave every castaway $2,000. That should solve the problem, he thought. Now we have way more money than before.

Of course, this did not solve the problem at all. What are the castaways going to buy? There are only so many fishing poles, canoes, coconuts, straw hats, etc. The castaways needed to *produce* more. They needed to produce more canoes, fishing poles, lean-tos, etc.

As you might expect, people started paying more for scarce food and prices rose sharply. There was far more money but no more goods—there were the same number of coconuts, canoes and fishing poles. The extra money didn't increase their ability to produce more goods.

This shows that printing money creates inflation, not prosperity. Increasing the money supply without increasing production solves nothing.

Now Back to the Real World

In the real world there are numerous examples of inflation causing economic catastrophes. Argentina is a perfect example. Between 1975 and 1990, Argentina kept printing money which led to triple-digit inflation, peaking at 200 percent in a single month—July 1989. They tried replacing their currency in 1985, calling it the austral instead of the peso, but it didn't work and inflation spiraled out of control.

The consequences for everyday Argentinians were devastating; poverty increased and economic growth was stunted. The manufacturing sector, once the backbone of Argentina's economy, entered a period of decline.

Inflation began to subside only when Argentina stopped printing money, reduced government spending and removed price controls. They reduced taxes, reformed labor laws and deregulated markets. They also improved access to credit and promoted investment. The lesson is clear: when governments attempt to "fix" economic problems by printing more money, they create inflation rather than prosperity.

The Federal Reserve: Modern-Day Robinson?

The story of Robinson printing money on his island is simplistic, but the Federal Reserve does essentially the same thing. The Federal Reserve, established in 1913, is America's central bank. When economic problems arise, they print more money. But just like on Robinson's island, printing money doesn't create anything real. The Fed cannot print factories or skilled workers or new inventions. They can only print paper. Real prosperity comes from making things people want, not from making more dollars.

This brings us to the fundamental questions. Why is economic freedom so important? Why does the United States have such a successful economy? What do we do differently than other counties? What is the nature of opportunity?

PART IV. The Bigger Questions

The United States thrives because of its entrepreneurial culture, competitive dynamics and willingness to embrace risk-taking. Freedom is the foundation of prosperity. Countries with the greatest freedom achieve the highest standards of living. Opportunities are not found; they are created. Free markets and capitalism have lifted more people out of poverty than any economic approach in history.

15 THE FREEDOM FACTOR

Economic freedom is simply freedom. It is the essential foundation for creating wealth and a high standard of living. Economic freedom enables people to start businesses, to work for themselves or to be employed by successful businesses. If a business is to be successful—to grow, to employ people and pay higher wages—it must operate in an environment of economic freedom.

History proves this point. Countries with the greatest amount of economic freedom are the most prosperous.

The correlation is unmistakable—economically free countries consistently achieve the highest standards of living, the longest lifespans and greatest poverty reduction. Appendix D includes a dramatic chart showing this relationship.

WHAT DOES ECONOMIC FREEDOM MEAN?

Economic freedom means that people are free to produce and trade with others. It is the right to control your own labor and property, free from coercion or compulsion. Individuals can work, produce, consume and invest however they choose—and keep the fruits of their labor.

When entrepreneurs can operate freely, they can build businesses that create jobs and drive growth. Economic freedom attracts investment and spurs innovation.

Entrepreneurs must be free to take risks and innovate, starting a business cannot be difficult, markets must remain open, the rule of law must be strong and property rights must be secure. Money must be sound, taxes reasonable and government's impact limited.

The Freedom to Innovate

Innovation happens because of freedom. People innovate only when they have the freedom to try things, to experiment and to fail. An environment of freedom enables innovation by allowing people to freely use their minds, their imaginations and their creativity.

A person who understands both freedom and its absence is Garry Kasparov, the Russian chess champion who lived under Soviet control before moving to the West. In his book *How Life Imitates Chess*, Kasparov writes:

> *Innovation requires freedom of thought, freedom of capital, and people who believe in changing the world. Yes, the free market can be cruel and it is by definition unequal. It has winners and losers. It also sparks the*

spirit of creativity that humanity desperately needs to flourish in our ever-increasing billions. Failure is an essential part of innovation and the free market.

Of every ten new companies, perhaps nine will fail in brutal Darwinian competition. A centrally-planned economy cannot imitate this engine of creative destruction because you cannot plan for failure. You cannot predestine which two college dropouts in a garage will produce the next Apple[16].

The successful technology entrepreneur, Peter Thiel, has ideas about freedom as well. He co-founded PayPal and Palantir Technologies and was an early investor in Facebook. Putting this philosophy into practice, Thiel developed the Thiel Fellowship for young people who want to build new things and not take the traditional path. The two-year program offers grants of $100,000 each for young people to skip college and pursue their ideas. The program connects these fellows with experienced founders, scientists and investors for support. The second tenet of the fellowship program states: "The freedom to get stuff done...to take on big risks. We're here to help, but we won't get in the way"[17].

Image by pexels

[16] Kasparov, Garry, *How Life Imitates Chess*, p. 48

[17] Thiel Fellowship, "Two years. $100,000. Some ideas can't wait.," https://thielfellowship.org/

Ease of Starting a Business

Economic freedom means that it is not overly burdensome to start a business. A favorable regulatory environment is important because too many regulations can stifle the creation of new businesses.

In some countries, entrepreneurs must jump through many hoops to get a business up and going. They must get a multitude of approvals, licenses, permits and pay fees. This bureaucratic maze can take months or even years, stifling entrepreneurial energy.

Open Markets

Economic freedom is the freedom to trade—to voluntarily exchange goods and services. You can produce goods and services and sell them freely to buyers. You are free to purchase the goods and services that you want.

Image bySauerArt from Pixabay

An open market is one in which there are few barriers to trade. Trade is voluntary and anyone can participate. A person or a company can conduct business easily, without bureaucratic hurdles, regulatory barriers or excessive paperwork. The licensing requirements are limited and there are minimal tariffs and streamlined regulations.

Secure Property Rights

Economic freedom means having the right to private property. You have the right to use your property as you choose. Property is not just real estate. Property includes your tools, your car, your money, your assets, your creations and intellectual property.

Perhaps you composed a song. That song is your property. A band cannot play that song without your permission or without payment to you. Without secure property rights, creators will find it difficult to benefit from their innovations.

Rule of Law

Economic freedom includes a legal system that protects your life as well as your property. Rule of law means that the laws are well-defined and fairly enforced, contracts are honored and corruption is absent.

Sound Money

Economic freedom includes having sound money. You can save money, invest and buy and sell goods with confidence. It means there will not be high inflation. Inflation is defined as the expansion in the money supply. Higher prices are the result of an expanding money supply.

High inflation erodes wages and erodes savings. It makes planning difficult when trying to manage a business. When money is rapidly going down in value, as it does with high inflation, making good decisions is quite challenging. Economic freedom is founded on having stable money as well as a government that is fiscally sound.

Reasonable Taxes

Economic freedom means the freedom to reap the rewards from your work efforts. You get to keep the money that you earned by serving your customers. Reasonable taxes encourage people to work and to produce. High taxes are a disincentive to work. The higher the taxes, the less a person gets to keep of the money that they earned.

Of course, we must pay taxes to fund the government

and pay for the activities that we want the government to perform. The balancing act is to pay for the government services that we require but also allow people to retain most of what they worked hard to earn. An economy thrives when citizens get to keep the bulk of their earnings, giving them both the incentive to work harder and the capital to spend and invest.

Limited Impact of Government

The cost and size of government impact economic freedom in a negative way. Federal spending consumes an increasing portion of our gross domestic product. For several decades, it accounted for about 18% of our GDP. Now it accounts for 23% of GDP[18]. Economic freedom has declined in the U.S. because of excessive government spending and increasing regulations, under both political parties.

If we include state and local government spending, the total government spending equals 38% of GDP. While this is significantly less than European countries like Germany (49%), Sweden and Denmark (49%), Italy (57%) and France (59%)[19], the upward trend in U.S. spending still represents a concerning decline in economic freedom.

Government debt is a problem that impacts freedom. Total U.S. government debt averaged around 40 to 50% of GDP for the last 25 years. In the last ten years, debt has been 85% of GDP[20]. Currently, debt is 123% of our GDP. This is a move in the wrong direction. Interest on our debt continues to escalate. Annual interest expense is now

---

[18] St. Louis Federal Reserve, https://fred.stlouisfed.org/series/FYONGDA188S

[19] OECD, Data, "General government spending," https://data.oecd.org/gga/general-government-spending.htm

[20] USA Facts, "How much debt does the US have?," https://usafacts.org/answers/how-much-debt-does-the-us-have/country/united-states/

greater than the defense budget[21].

Government regulations need reform. While we certainly need regulations, the more difficult question is how much is too much? New regulations are put in place every year but few old regulations ever go away. As a result, the pile of regulations gets larger and larger.

Measuring Freedom

Economic freedom can be measured. The Fraser Institute and the Heritage Foundation have each developed indices that measure economic freedom. They track several factors: openness to trade, property rights, regulations, government size, open markets, corruption, taxes, investment and the ease of starting a business. The top five countries for economic freedom according to Heritage are: Singapore, Switzerland, Ireland, Taiwan and Luxembourg. These freedom indices are described in more detail in Appendix D.

---

[21] https://budget.house.gov/press-release/interest-costs-surpass-national-defense-and-medicare-spending

16 WHY AMERICA THRIVES

The United States' exceptional economic success stems from a combination of entrepreneurial culture and economic freedom that spark innovation and productivity.

Our standard of living is higher than almost anywhere in the world. This has been going on for decades. It is not a new phenomenon.

What do we mean by successful? In this context, being successful means creating a high standard of living for the people. It means being prosperous. We are not talking about the top five percent who are indeed wealthy, we are talking about the United States as a whole, where the average person enjoys a relatively high standard of living.

Prosperity is a good thing because it means we have more money and resources to pay for healthcare, to clean up the environment and to discover life-saving drugs. We can afford new labor-saving devices that enable parents to spend more time with their children.

Prosperity and Wealth

Many people do not understand *why* the United States is a prosperous or a wealthy country. Where does wealth come from? How is it created? Many believe that wealth is mostly inherited, passed down from generation to generation. This is not correct.

Forbes magazine lists the wealthiest 400 people in the United States. It confirms that 70 percent of these people became wealthy through their own efforts by building businesses[22]. Only 30 percent are wealthy because they inherited money from their parents or grandparents.

Almost all wealth is generated by entrepreneurs creating and growing successful companies. Wealth comes from discipline, hard work and imagination. Jeff Bezos founded Amazon and became wealthy. Bill Gates founded Microsoft and became wealthy. Elon Musk founded SpaceX, PayPal, Tesla and several other ventures, making him the wealthiest person on the planet.

Athletes and entertainers like Tiger Woods and J.K. Rowling also built wealth through talent and hard work, but the real wealth creation happens when entrepreneurs build companies.

Wealth erodes over time. This explains why inherited wealth rarely lasts beyond three generations. Without the entrepreneurial drive that created it, money simply gets spent rather than multiplied. The personal traits that successful entrepreneurs embody—a burning desire to succeed, an ethic of hard work—are difficult to pass on to children who grow up wealthy.

WHY *IS* THE USA SO SUCCESSFUL?

What are the reasons for our success? Is it because we have abundant natural resources? Is it because we have smart people? Is it because of our entrepreneurs? Is it because of our government?

The United States does have many advantages—natural resources, educated people, good infrastructure.

---

[22] Forbes, www.forbes.com/sites/gigizamora/2023/10/03/the-2023-forbes-400-self-made-score-from-silver-spooners-to-bootstrappers/

But as we'll see, these alone do not create prosperity. Countries with these advantages often remain poor. The difference is economic freedom and entrepreneurship. Let's explore why these factors do not explain America's success.

Natural Resources

First, let's consider natural resources. The United States does have substantial resources: oil and gas, rich forests, farmland and navigable rivers. But so do other countries.

Three countries that have an abundance of natural resources but have poor economic growth and a low quality of life are Russia, Venezuela and Argentina. These countries are rich, and I mean really rich, in resources. Russia has vast reserves of oil and gas. In addition, the country has extensive mineral deposits. Russia has huge expanses of land, not every acre is good for farming but it still possesses vast amounts of good farmland.

Image by -MemoryCatcher from Pixabay

Despite having these resources, the average Russian earns only $14,000 per year, one-sixth of an American worker[23]. Their population is shrinking and life expectancy is decreasing. The people are poor and not particularly free.

Venezuela has the world's largest oil reserves yet its

[23] Trading Economics, "Wages," https://tradingeconomics.com/russia/wages

people flee to neighboring countries to escape poverty and hunger.

In 1920, Argentina was among the world's ten wealthiest nations. Today it ranks 145th in economic freedom and 40 percent of its people live in poverty[24]. The country had many valuable economic assets, including thriving farming and cattle industries. The political system changed in the 1930s and everything slid downhill from there. How can you go from the top 10 to number 145? That is not easy to do. Argentina still possesses a wealth of resources. What is wrong here?

Image by acuatro by Pixabay

Argentina will be an interesting country to watch over the next few years. A new president, Javier Milei, was elected in December 2023. He has been instituting many significant free market reforms. Within his first six months, Milei eliminated 5,000 government regulations, cut government spending by 35 percent and began privatizing inefficient state-owned enterprises.

The results have been promising: inflation fell from a staggering 211 percent annually in December 2023 to 47 percent by April 2025 and the Argentine peso has stabilized after years of decline[25]. While still in the early stages, positive growth is expected in 2025.

---

[24] The Heritage Foundation, 2024 Index of Economic Freedom, www.heritage.org/index/pages/report

[25] Trading Economics, Argentina Inflation Rate, https://tradingeconomics.com/argentina/inflation-cpi

What makes Argentina such a compelling case study is that its problems were never about resources—the country has some of the world's richest farmland, significant oil and gas deposits and abundant mineral wealth. Decades of protectionist policies, excessive regulation, currency controls and state intervention in the economy transformed one of the world's richest countries into economic failure. This stark example demonstrates that natural resources alone cannot create prosperity without the economic freedom to utilize them effectively.

What about countries that have very few resources—like Hong Kong and Japan? They have extremely successful economies and few natural resources. Natural resources are certainly a good thing, but a country does not become wealthy just because it has natural resources. We can take natural resources off the table as a reason for a country being wealthy.

Smart People

Many countries have brilliant scientists and engineers. Russia graduates thousands of PhDs in mathematics, physics and engineering every year. Instead of creating wealth at home, many of Russia's brightest minds emigrate to countries with economic freedom. Russia does not have an environment for them to flourish. That makes all the difference.

What matters is how a country utilizes its resources, whether these are natural resources or smart people. Does it have incentives for these people to exercise their minds and to flourish?

Americans Work Harder

Americans work significantly more hours than Europeans, and there's a clear economic reason why. The average employee in the U.S. works 1800 hours per year. In France they work 1500 hours. In Sweden and Norway, people work slightly more than 1400 hours and in Germany, they work 1350 hours per year[26].

Workers in Europe don't get to keep as much of their pay because they are taxed at much higher rates. Americans retain 72 percent of their gross pay, while the typical German worker keeps just 52 percent of their earnings and French workers keep only 53 percent. These massive tax differences—often 15 to 20 percentage points higher in Europe—reduce incentives to work longer hours or seek higher-paying positions.

Flexible Labor Markets

The U.S. has flexible labor markets. This is very different than in Europe. Europe has stringent labor laws and restrictive regulations that impede job mobility. It is difficult to fire people in Europe for a variety of reasons. As a result, companies are more hesitant to hire people because if business turns down, they will not have the flexibility to move people to part time or to lay people off. This makes building a business more difficult.

Workers in the United States are mobile. They move from one job to another more frequently than do European workers. The average American stays in a job for just four years. The average European stays in a job about 11 years[27]. This mobility allows workers to move to higher-paying positions, driving up wages as companies compete for talent.

Vibrant Venture Capital

The United States has both sophisticated financial markets and the world's most robust venture capital

---

[26] OECD, Stat, "Average annual hours actually worked per worker," https://stats.oecd.org/Index.aspx?DataSetCode=ANHRS

[27] Bureau of Labor Statistics, "Employee Tenure in 2024," https://www.bls.gov/news.release/pdf/tenure.pdf

system. The financial markets experienced disruption during the 2008 crisis, but they have proven resilient and continue to attract more capital than any other country. A stable monetary system provides the foundation for entrepreneurial growth.

The numbers tell the story: America deploys six times more venture capital funding than all European countries combined. The U.S. has 2,361 active VC firms managing $271 billion compared to Europe's 200 firms managing just $44 billion[28]. Raising capital from angel investors has also become easier and more commonplace across the United States.

This capital gap helps explain why the U.S. produces more unicorns (billion-dollar startups) than Europe. Silicon Valley alone generates more high-growth technology companies than all European tech hubs combined. This abundance of risk capital enables American entrepreneurs to scale quickly and compete more effectively.

Other Positive Factors

The United States has additional positive factors that help our country to flourish, to generate wealth and to create a high standard of living. Good government, protection of property rights and rule of law are essential.

Our regulatory framework, while not perfect, allows far more business flexibility than European systems. However, each year thousands of new regulations are added that negatively impact business growth. We certainly need regulations, but too many can strangle businesses and reduce their ability to grow and create jobs.

Our tax system is certainly not perfect, but it is

---

[28] Crunchbase News, Oct. 19, 2023, https://news.crunchbase.com/venture/europe-leads-us-startup-vc-gray-equidam/

reasonably good compared to other countries. The U.S. system encourages people to work and companies to produce. This is particularly true when contrasted to Europe.

The United States has excellent universities that produce basic research. Many tech companies have started up by licensing university research, developing new products and commercializing new technologies.

The United States is comprised of 50 states. These states compete to attract businesses that create jobs. Businesses move to those states where talented employees and other resources are available, where the tax situation is favorable and where regulations are less stringent. In the early 2020s a number of high-profile companies moved from California to Texas for these reasons. Notable firms include Chevron, Oracle, Tesla, X, SpaceX, Charles Schwab, CBRE, Hewlett Packard Enterprise and McKesson.

The United States is successful because it has economic freedom, an abundance of entrepreneurs and a culture that embraces risk-taking.

A Culture of Risk-Taking

The United States possesses a distinct culture that embraces risk-taking and individualism, unlike many other developed nations. While countries like Japan and Germany value conformity, planning and security, America celebrates bold innovation and entrepreneurial ventures. Americans generally admire those who take risks and strike out on their own, creating an environment where entrepreneurship is respected rather than viewed with skepticism.

This spirit of individualism translates directly into economic outcomes. Our willingness to take risks encourages more business startups, innovative technologies and disruptive business models. When entrepreneurs create new products and services, they generate real wealth—not just for themselves but for society through better goods, services and employment opportunities.

This risk-taking spirit, combined with economic freedom, creates an ecosystem where new ventures can flourish. This explains the significant gap in entrepreneurial activity between the United States and Europe.

COMPARING THE U.S. TO EUROPE

How does the U.S. stack up to Europe in terms of income and standard of living? The answer is that we are remarkably better.

Two measures contrast the incomes and wealth of countries: the average wage and GDP per capita. The average annual wage in the U.S. was $80,115 in 2023, compared to $65,719 in Germany, $59,087 in France and $57,617 in the United Kingdom. American workers earn 22 percent to 40 percent more than their European counterparts.

The U.S. produces more goods and services than any country in the world. This is measured by gross domestic product, or GDP. To compare countries of different sizes, it is best to look at GDP per person (GDP per capita).

The following chart shows 2024 GDP per capita for major economies:

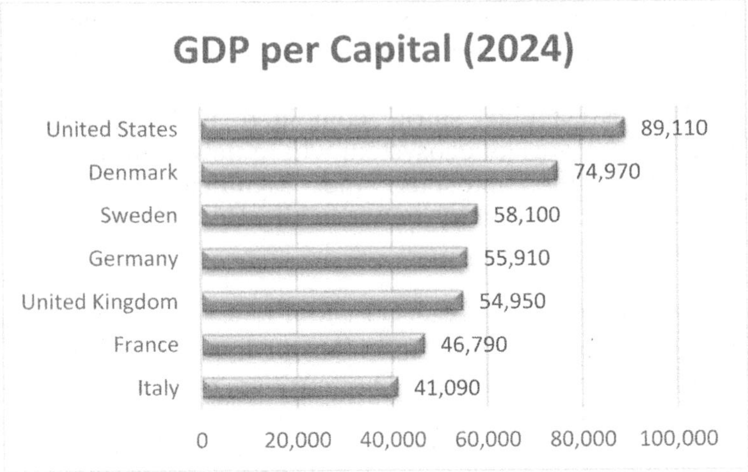

Source: International Monetary Fund

Poorer countries include Spain at $36,190, Portugal at $30,000 and Greece at $25,760[29].

Compared to Germany and Sweden, the U.S. GDP per capita was 55 percent greater. Compared to France it was 89 percent greater and compared to Italy, it was more than double. These differences are substantial.

The numbers tell the story. The United States is the most productive country in the world. We produce more in absolute terms and we produce more per person.

When comparing economies internationally, economists often use Purchasing Power Parity (PPP) to account for cost-of-living differences. PPP adjusts for price differences between countries, giving a more accurate picture of what people can actually buy with their income. Even when adjusted for PPP, the United States maintains a substantial advantage over European countries.

---

[29] Statistics Times, www.statisticstimes.com/economy/european-countries-by-gdp-per-capita.php

In 2023, U.S. GDP per capita at PPP was approximately $76,400, compared to Germany at $69,206, France at $58,318 and the United Kingdom at $58,225[30]. This means that even after accounting for cost-of-living differences, Americans enjoy 20 percent to 35 percent higher real purchasing power than citizens of major European economies.

Cultural Attitudes Toward Entrepreneurship

Beyond economic policies and regulations, there are profound cultural differences that shape how entrepreneurs are regarded.

Europeans view entrepreneurs differently than do Americans. Americans generally admire entrepreneurs. This is not the case in Europe. The British research institute, IREF, revealed that "Europeans do not see business and entrepreneurship with admiration. According to a sentiment analysis of media coverage, only about 17 percent of press coverage in Germany portrays entrepreneurship positively, compared to 39 percent in the United States"[31].

In addition, Europe has fewer entrepreneurs per capita. "Europe has only 0.8 super-entrepreneurs per million people, compared to 3.1 in the U.S."[32]. Europe is large and well-educated with a good standard of living. However, their productivity is sluggish and cumbersome regulations negatively impact growth.

---

[30] World Bank Group, GDP per capita, PPP, https://data.worldbank.org/indicator/NY.GDP.PCAP.PP.CD?locations=EU

[31] The Institute for Research in Economic and Fiscal Issues, "Fiscal competition and economic freedom" https://en.irefeurope.org/publications/online-articles/article/why-does-europe-suffer-from-an-entrepreneurship-crisis/#sdfootnote7sym

[32] ibid

Innovation and Technology Gaps

Europe is lagging in some critical technology sectors—artificial intelligence, biotech, semiconductors and EV battery technology. Despite having talented workforces and strong educational systems, European countries have not created the same dynamic environment for technology advancement as the United States. This contributes to their lower productivity and slower economic growth.

The economic dynamism in the U.S. stems from a robust entrepreneurial culture combined with economic freedom—a powerful combination that Europe has struggled to replicate.

Conclusion: America's Economic Edge

What distinguishes the United States is its entrepreneurial ecosystem. Americans work longer hours with more flexible labor markets, move between jobs more readily and benefit from financial systems that fund innovation. The regulatory and tax environments, while not perfect, create incentives for growth and productivity.

Most importantly, America embraces risk-taking and entrepreneurship, creating a society where innovation thrives. Americans celebrate those who take chances and create new products and services. This entrepreneurial spirit, combined with economic freedom, explains why American workers earn 40 percent more than British workers and nearly double what Italians make, and why the U.S. maintains its position as the world's most productive economy.

Countries that want to improve their citizens' standard of living should reduce barriers to entrepreneurship and cultivate a culture that rewards innovation and risk-taking. Economic freedom remains the most reliable path to prosperity.

Economic freedom is declining worldwide. Three consecutive years of decline have pushed the global average to its lowest level since 2001. Even the United States has seen its freedom score drop to 25th. The erosion of economic freedom—from increased regulation, government intervention and mounting public debt—threatens what makes America's economy work.

Economic freedom is critical for America's success and the country needs to remember this. Our advantages in entrepreneurship, innovation and productivity will only thrive in an environment of economic freedom. Countries that embrace freedom will prosper. Those that don't will fall behind.

17 THE NATURE OF OPPORTUNITY

Opportunities do not simply exist in the world waiting to be discovered. Entrepreneurs create them.

Opportunities are not self-evident. An opportunity is not like a $100 bill lying on the sidewalk to be found by the first passerby. An opportunity is something that develops from inside the person. Opportunities depend on the knowledge and skills of the person. They are internal and subjective. An opportunity for one person may not be an opportunity for another person.

For example, a broken-down car is an opportunity for a mechanic who has experience repairing automobiles. If someone does not have those skills, the broken-down car is not an opportunity for them.

Image by DokaRyan from Pixabay

You can offer someone a job and that *does*

give them an opportunity. However, that job offer exists because of the person's education, skills and experience—their internal capabilities. Without those skills, there is no job offer.

The story of Airbnb demonstrates how opportunities emerge from within entrepreneurs. When a big design conference came to San Francisco, local hotels were fully booked. Designers Brian Chesky and Joe Gebbia were not searching for an existing opportunity in the hotel industry, but they recognized potential where others did not—in their own apartment. They bought a few air mattresses and created a website offering "Air Bed and Breakfast" to people going to the conference.

What's remarkable isn't just their success, because millions of people had spare rooms. The physical assets existed everywhere. Traditional business thinking might have been, "The hospitality market is saturated with established hotel chains—there's no opportunity here." But the opportunity wasn't lying on the sidewalk waiting to be found; it emerged from the founders' unique perspective and decision to turn spare bedrooms into affordable accommodations.

This example demonstrates how entrepreneurs do not just respond to obvious opportunities—they generate entirely new ones by connecting the dots differently. The opportunity was not in the spare rooms that existed all along; it was in the entrepreneurs' minds that connected those rooms to a market platform that had not previously existed.

Entrepreneurs test ideas relentlessly. They spot a potential solution, try it, learn from what doesn't work, and adjust. Many attempts fail, but each failure teaches them something about the market, customer preferences, price and other factors. They don't get it right the first time—they iterate, pivot and refine until they find what works. When entrepreneurs push on the world, they can generate opportunities.

Slack is an excellent example of a company that shifted its focus after a failure, and found a way to generate a new opportunity. Slack started out by building a game called *Glitch*, an online game designed for multiplayers. The company had raised $17 million in venture capital and had 40 employees. However, the game failed. It was too complicated, not fast enough and generally not fun. It did not gain the user base that the company had hoped.

The team was scattered around North America. To enable real-time collaboration, the engineers developed an internal messaging tool. This tool morphed into Slack's suite of communication tools. Eventually, the platform gained popularity because it was user-friendly with robust capabilities: it enabled chat, file sharing, voice and video calls, and more—it made users more productive. It revolutionized how remote teams communicated and collaborated.

Image by mikhail-nilov from Pexels

Slack adapted to the changing needs of business and transitioned from a failed game company to a new product category. The transition required persistence and determination. Today Slack has more than 10 million daily active users. The company was acquired by Salesforce in 2020 for $27.7 billion.

Try things, shift, try again. That is how entrepreneurs generate opportunity.

The Slack example illustrates a key principle: opportunities don't exist waiting to be discovered. The

Slack founders didn't stumble across a ready-made opportunity. They generated it through their unique technical skills, market insight and willingness to experiment. Opportunities are created by a person's knowledge, skills and determination to solve problems.

Equality

Few topics in discussions about capitalism ignite more passionate debate than equality and opportunity. Critics argue that capitalism produces too much inequality, while proponents emphasize the opportunities it creates. These perspectives often miss the point because they address fundamentally different concepts: equality of outcome versus equality of opportunity.

Equality of Outcome

Equality of outcome means everyone gets the same result regardless of effort or choices. This requires taking money from successful people and giving it to others.

The problem with equal outcomes is simple: someone must enforce them. That means government must limit what successful people can earn and redistribute their wealth. This treats wealth like a pie to be sliced up instead of something entrepreneurs create from scratch.

Reducing poverty is important, but guaranteeing equal results destroys what drives entrepreneurs to innovate. Why work harder and take risks if everyone gets the same reward? Free markets don't care about your background—they care about what you deliver.

History shows that countries that enforce equal outcomes don't make everyone equally wealthy—they make everyone equally poor. Everyone gets an equal share of less.

Equality of Opportunity

Opportunities are created by entrepreneurs. Their vision and determination drive them to build a business. Since opportunities are developed internally, they cannot be given to someone else. As we saw with Airbnb and Slack, opportunities emerged from the founders' internal capabilities, not from external resources that could be allocated or apportioned.

The key point is that opportunities aren't objects sitting somewhere that can be handed out; they are generated by individuals. Unlike jobs or money, opportunities can't be distributed because they depend on the unique combination of knowledge, skills and perspective that each person brings. This is why government programs that claim to 'provide opportunities' miss the mark—they can provide resources or training, but the opportunity itself must be generated by the individual.

There is a way to help people generate real opportunities. That way is education—whether it's college, trade school, night classes, apprenticeships or online courses. When people get more education, they gain more knowledge, skills and competence that enable them to create opportunities.

Understanding that opportunities are generated by individuals—shaped by their unique perspectives and knowledge—underscores why economic freedom is so important. A free society creates the conditions where more people can pursue their ideas and build businesses that create value.

At its core, entrepreneurial opportunity requires freedom—freedom to take risks, freedom to fail, freedom to try again. Opportunities cannot be given out like government benefits. They come from within—from people's knowledge and skills.

18 MUSINGS ON CAPITALISM

Capitalism has created more prosperity than any economic approach in history. Capitalism embraces uncertainty and no one is in charge—the opposite of what most people would think would be effective.

The Nature of Capitalism

What exactly do we mean by capitalism? How do we define it? Capitalism refers to an economy that is based on private property and free markets. It is characterized by voluntary transactions between people.

Capitalism is an economic process, not a social system. It doesn't solve social problems like education or mental health. Market capitalism is about business and free enterprise.

Some criticize capitalism because it is profit-seeking or because it falls short of utopia. This misses the point entirely. The question isn't whether capitalism achieves perfection—no human institution does. The question is whether it delivers better results than any alternative. Market economies have consistently improved lives and raised living standards worldwide while making the poor better off.

You do not have to agree with the idea of capitalism. You may prefer socialism. Before forming your opinion, you should have an accurate concept of how free-market capitalism actually works.

Capitalism is Not a "System"

Capitalism is not planned or organized from the top down. No one is in charge. Rather, capitalism operates from the bottom up, without central coordination. It emerges from millions of individual decisions, which makes it resilient and adaptable.

Technically, capitalism is not a system at all. "Systems" are designed and structured by someone and a person or group oversees the operation to achieve specific outcomes. Think library system, transit system, air conditioning system, postal system. Capitalism simply emerges when people are free to interact and trade.

Capitalism is the only economic approach in human history which is based on free exchange and win-win trade and interactions between people. Entrepreneurs make capitalism happen by starting companies, building companies and inventing new products. They also hire people and create jobs.

The Morality of Free Markets

Free markets and voluntary exchange empower the individual. Empowering the individual is a profoundly moral thing. Under capitalism, people have the freedom to use their abilities and judgment to make a living for themselves and their families. This freedom to choose is fundamental to human dignity and fulfillment. The individual is at the center, not the group and not the state.

Free markets are built, not on coercion, but on voluntary interactions between people. Prior to market economies, people typically had to use coercion to become wealthy. Capitalism works by serving others—

businesses succeed only by satisfying their customers, which improves people's lives. This foundation of voluntary exchange makes the free market morally superior to all other economic approaches.

Capitalism proves its value through results. When people are free to start businesses and trade voluntarily, it creates wealth and drives innovation.

Customer Sovereignty

Capitalism is based on customer sovereignty—the idea that customers are the ultimate decision-makers. Businesses exist for only one reason—to provide value for their customers. If a company does not provide real value for its customers, it will eventually go out of business.

Companies come and companies go. New technologies are invented and old technologies become obsolete. This continuous process occurs because companies are relentlessly trying to serve customers' needs in the best possible way and thereby earn a profit.

To stay competitive, businesses must evolve and adjust. This necessity drives capitalism's most dynamic feature—innovation.

Innovation

Capitalism's greatest strength is that it encourages trial and error. This process produces innovation and growth. It does this because entrepreneurs have both the freedom to experiment and the incentive to succeed. This drives a steady stream of new products and services as competitors strive to serve customers better and capture market share.

Capitalism Reduces Poverty

Consider this remarkable fact: 1.35 billion people moved out of extreme poverty in the last 30 years. In 1990, 37.4% of the world's population lived in extreme poverty, on less than $2.15 per day. Thirty years later, only 9.7% live in extreme poverty[33]. This is an unprecedented achievement.

More countries have adopted market capitalism. Even China has embraced free market practices—allowing private businesses, self-employment and replacing collective farming with household-based farming. The results were dramatic: agricultural productivity soared as farmers gained the freedom to make their own decisions about crops, methods and timing. Many became entrepreneurs, starting small businesses and food processing operations. Previously, farmers started work at collective farms at the sound of a whistle with no incentive to innovate. Now some begin tending their private farms before sunrise because they keep the fruits of their labor.

The global reduction in poverty did not occur only in China. Countries like India, Bangladesh and Vietnam have dramatically reduced poverty through market-oriented reforms. South Asia reduced extreme poverty from 50% in 1990 to 9% in 2019[34]. The pattern is clear: free markets reduce poverty.

Concluding Remarks

Market capitalism has brought Americans the highest standard of living in the world. Americans have become complacent about this golden goose.

We take for granted that entrepreneurs will continue to innovate and solve our problems—new treatments for diseases, breakthrough technologies, solutions to problems we have not even identified.

It is human nature to assume that these benefits will be permanent, especially since they have existed for decades. Many people believe that these advantages will

---

[33] Our World in Data, "Global Extreme Poverty," https://ourworldindata.org/extreme-poverty

[34] ibid

remain even if we put shackles on free-market capitalism. This thinking is fueled by economic misunderstandings—like thinking corporate profits are excessive when they average only 7%. The United States is the wealthiest country in human history with prosperity that surpasses all others. Americans need to appreciate why we are rich and not become complacent about it.

The United States has 330 million people from all parts of the world—different backgrounds, beliefs and religions. People still want to come here. Why do you think that is? One primary reason is our economic freedom and opportunity. The United States is a good place to live, to work, to raise a family and to have a quality life.

Appendices

Appendix A: Traits of Entrepreneurs

Appendix B: Why Do We Have Corporations?

Appendix C: Why Do We Need Wall Street?

Appendix D: Measuring Economic Freedom

Appendix E: Robots and Job

Appendix F: Artificial Intelligence

APPENDIX A: TRAITS OF ENTREPRENEURS

What Makes them Tick?

Anyone can be an entrepreneur. There is no entrance exam. You don't need a college degree. You don't need a resume. There are no qualifications. There is no test. There are no barriers to entry. There are no limits.

Entrepreneurship is not for the faint of heart. It takes courage to be an entrepreneur. It takes guts to make sales calls. You might get rejected. Entrepreneurs have to hire and fire people, and firing someone is never easy.

Building a business means overcoming obstacles. Entrepreneurs face problems daily. Cash flow dries up, customers complain, suppliers let you down. Equipment breaks, employees quit, or customers don't pay. Determination and persistence are what determine success. The essence of entrepreneurship is being unreasonable. Entrepreneurs do not accept the world as it is—they try to change it. As George Bernard Shaw wrote in *Man and Superman*:

> *The reasonable man adapts himself to the world; the unreasonable one persists in trying to adapt the world to himself. Therefore, all progress depends on the unreasonable man.*

Entrepreneurs question the established ways of doing things. They might see an opportunity where a more reasonable person sees obstacles. Their goals may be highly unrealistic. A reasonable person may think of all the reasons *not* to move forward.

Entrepreneurs take action. They try, fail and try again. When obstacles appear, they push through. It's about taking risks and forging ahead.

What Are Their Personalities?

The personalities of entrepreneurs are all over the map—introverts, extroverts, brilliant and average. Some are shy; some are very outgoing. In my experience, the average ones often do better. The brilliant ones can get any job they want and are often averse to risk. Despite these differences, they all share certain essential character traits:

- Relentless determination
- Passion
- Resilience
- Not afraid to fail

Determination is the quintessential trait of every successful entrepreneur. You don't have to be highly educated. You don't have to be super smart. But you must be relentlessly determined. Unreasonable persistence might be another term for this essential quality.

Passion is a given. Entrepreneurs must be passionate about developing their new product, about building their businesses and about serving their customers. Without passion an entrepreneur is destined to fail. In building Apple, Steve Jobs embodied the extreme passion that is necessary to push through all the obstacles, missteps and challenges that entrepreneurs face. Jobs stressed the importance of passion:

> *People say you have to have a lot of passion for what you are doing and it is totally true. And the reason is because it's so hard that if you don't, any rational person would give up. It is really hard. And you have to do it over a sustained period of time. So, if you don't love it...if you're not having fun doing it and you don't really love it, you are going to give up*[35].

Entrepreneurs are resilient. When they get knocked down, they get back up. Whether it's a failed product launch, the loss of a major customer or a key employee quitting, they pivot and adapt.

Image by DS 30 from Pixabay

Entrepreneurs are not afraid to fail. They don't expect to fail, of course, but they are not afraid to try. They are willing to take the risk.

These traits are not inherent—they are conscious decisions. Entrepreneurs decide to persevere, they decide to be determined, they decide to face obstacles head on. They decide to work fearlessly to find a

[35] Steve Jobs, *Interview by Kara Swisher and Walt Mossberg at the D5 Conference*, May 30, 2007.

way forward. These are deliberate choices.

James Dyson is a perfect example of these qualities. He epitomizes the unreasonable persistence and determination of an entrepreneur. As a young man in England, Dyson pursued architecture and was interested in functional design and engineering. He was a tinkerer and an inventor. To fund his work, Dyson's wife supported the family and three children by working as an art teacher. They went into debt, using their house as collateral for loans.

The idea for a better vacuum cleaner clicked when he visited a sawmill and noticed the mill was removing dust using cyclonic separators. He had been frustrated by his Hoover vacuum cleaner that often got clogged; plus, the bag was not reusable. Over five years of trial and error, Dyson tried out 5,127 prototypes of the vacuum cleaner. Eventually, it worked to his satisfaction[36].

Dyson found that he was fighting an uphill battle since the market for selling replacement bags was quite profitable. No one wanted to manufacture or sell his product. After initially licensing his technology to established companies, he decided to maintain control of his invention and started his own manufacturing business. The company became hugely successful.

James Dyson invented other products over the years but his path to success has not been without failure. He

[36] https://www.dyson.com/james-dyson

overcame obstacles that would cause most people to quit. Dyson stated "Success tells you nothing. Failure is interesting—it's part of making progress. You never learn from success, but you do learn from failure"[37].

Why did Dyson start his own company? Why didn't he just get a job designing new products at an engineering firm? He could have had a steady salary with significantly less financial risk.

Why Do Entrepreneurs Start Companies?

Some think it's because they have good ideas. Heck, anyone who ever took a shower had an idea. Some think it's to get rich, which is certainly a motivation for some. But the fundamental reason most entrepreneurs start companies is that they absolutely do not want to work for anyone else.

True entrepreneurs create their companies because it is their life's work. It is their art. One might call it performance art. Their goal is to build something. Their objective is to improve their customers' lives in some way. It is about the purity of effort. Yes, they want to make money; of course, they do. They had better make money or they will not succeed.

Entrepreneurs are about freedom. The freedom to work for themselves. The freedom to start and build a business the way that they want to. The freedom to make mistakes. The freedom to fail and to begin again. Determination is their driving force and it is complemented by passion, resilience and the ability to stare down failure.

---

[37] ibid

APPENDIX B: WHY DO WE NEED WALL STREET?

Wall Street is the center of the financial markets for the United States and for much of the world. Finance plays a very productive role in growing our economy, making us better off. Many Americans don't understand the role of the companies and institutions that are known as Wall Street.

What is Wall Street?

Wall Street includes commercial banks, mutual funds, investment banks, insurance companies, stock exchanges and more. A broader definition includes commodity traders, hedge funds and currency traders. These institutions are based in New York City for the most part. With global markets, these firms could be located anywhere, but they are still referred to as "Wall Street."

Why Everyone Hates Wall Street

Everybody hates Wall Street, right? It doesn't create anything. It just leaches off the rest of us. It is a parasite. Wall Street is like a slumlord in pin-striped suits. They perform useless activities. Plus, the markets are rigged. Bankers and speculators get wealthy at other people's expense. Is Wall Street really that bad? What is the story? Does Wall Street do *anything* good or productive?

First, Wall Street deserves criticism for the financial crisis of 2008. Firms created and sold complex, high-risk financial products with undisclosed conflicts of interest. There was a failure of regulators, credit rating agencies and the market itself to rein in the excesses. Regulators failed to keep pace with complex new instruments.

The institutional investors who purchased these products also bear responsibility. Many pension funds, insurance companies and others chasing higher yields—failed to conduct proper due diligence. Some bought despite the warning signs, because of competitive pressures to achieve high returns.

So what does Wall Street actually do for the rest of us?

Wall Street and You

Wall Street impacts your life in many ways. Do you have a credit card? A car loan? A mortgage for your house? Do you carry insurance? Do you have a retirement plan? Wall Street is responsible for those financial products.

Why do we need Wall Street? The short answer is to facilitate saving and investing for individuals and to provide capital for businesses. People rely on Wall Street to safeguard their money and to provide a range of investment products. Wall Street creates markets where people can buy and sell stocks, bonds, insurance and commodities.

FINANCE THE GROWTH OF INDUSTRY

The primary role of Wall Street is to allocate capital and finance the growth of industries. Without this capital, most of the companies that employ Americans could not exist.

Farmers Use Wall Street

Farming is a good example of an industry that Wall Street helps. Farmers use Wall Street for three primary reasons: equipment loans, insurance and reducing the risks of price changes.

Farmers use many kinds of heavy equipment and this equipment is not cheap. Your basic John Deere tractor has a base price of $300,000. A large fancy model will run you $700,000. Farmers also need specialized equipment depending on what crops they grow. They need equipment to till the soil, a planter to plant seeds ($310,000). They need harvesting equipment and perhaps a combine ($400,000). A combine "combines" the process of harvesting and separating the grain in one step.

They might also need an auger, a sprayer, a raker and irrigation equipment. Farms must replace equipment on a regular basis. As a result, farmers need loans to buy or lease new equipment. Add it all up, and the numbers get big fast. The average farm has $1.3 million in debt[38].

[38] Farm Progress, Tyler Harris, "Report: Average farm debt rises over $1.3 million," May 25, 2018,

Buying and Selling of Risk

Farming is risky business. Many factors are uncontrollable, like weather, disease, insects, lack of rain as well as fluctuating market prices. Taking risks in a prudent way is essential to building a business. If we don't take risks, we don't grow. Wall Street enables the buying and selling of risk.

Insurance is a way to reduce risk that we are all familiar with. Insurance is simply a pooling of risk. Farmers need insurance that covers the equipment in case of breakdown. Farmers can even get animal collision insurance. (You probably don't have coverage for that.) Farmers need liability insurance in case employees are injured on the job. They need building insurance for their barns, sheds, garages and grain silos. Wall Street provides all these different types of insurance.

An innovative way for a farmer to reduce the risk of price changes is by using a futures contract. The farmer can lock in today's price of corn and then ship the corn in six months. The farmer is not trying to speculate; he is reducing his risk of loss.

Let's say that the current price of corn is $10 per bushel and the farmer is happy with that price. But it will be six months before he can grow and sell his corn. What if the price goes down to $7? The farmer will lose money. How can he lock in the $10 price? He locks it in by selling a futures contract. He makes a deal with a speculator (through a Wall Street firm). The contract specifies that the farmer will deliver a certain number of bushels of corn and he will be paid $10 per bushel. The speculator is making a bet that the price of corn will go up. The futures contract removes the risk of a price drop for the farmer. Farming is risky enough so reducing the risk of a price drop is a good thing.

---

https://www.farmprogress.com/management/report-average-farm-debt-rises-over-13-million

Capital for Businesses

Financiers helped create Silicon Valley and the technology companies that invent nifty new products and services. Every year thousands of start-up companies are financed by venture capital firms that provide capital.

Facebook raised capital through the Wall Street firm Goldman Sachs which allowed the company to expand its operations and to hire more employees. Facebook also needed cash to expand internationally—not just to Europe, but to Russia and China. Facebook raised $2.2 billion in capital in 19 rounds of financing before its public offering in 2012. Now called Meta Platforms, the company employs 74,000 people.

Wall Street also helps successful companies go public and list their stock on a stock exchange. When a company like Uber goes public, your retirement fund can buy shares, and Uber gets the capital to expand to new cities. This enables companies to access capital for growth.

Beyond equity financing, Wall Street provides loans that businesses need—for equipment, inventory, facilities and major projects like new factories. Financial firms pool savings and transform them into business loans.

LOANS FOR PEOPLE

Think about how your life would be different without loans. Loans enable people to spend money now instead of waiting until later. Maybe a father wants to put in a swimming pool for his family to enjoy. If he waited until he could afford the entire cost of the pool, it might be many years later. He would like to get a loan now so the family can enjoy the fun times in the swimming pool while the kids are still young.

Without loans, you would need to save $450,000 before buying a house. It would take you decades or more to save up that much money. What if you want to get married and have a family? You want to live in the house *now*!

Before buying a car, you would have to save up enough money to buy the whole car. Do you rent an apartment? Where did the apartment come from? Even your apartment building was financed with loans. So, we do need Wall Street.

INVESTMENTS FOR PEOPLE

Wall Street offers thousands of different investments. Anyone with a retirement account, such as an IRA or a 401(k) account, benefits from Wall Street. Having choices means you can invest the way that makes sense for you. Mutual funds and exchange traded funds (ETFs) are available to suit almost any investment objective. If you want to invest in a specific industry sector, mutual funds and ETFs are an excellent way to go. You can invest in a fund that specializes in clean energy or oil and gas or foreign stocks.

Need to sell some stock to pay for your kid's college? You can do it in seconds, not weeks. If you are 30 and want aggressive growth, or you're 60 and want steady income, Wall Street has products for both.

Wall Street provides the loans, investments and capital that power the American economy. Without it, businesses would struggle to grow, buying a home would be more difficult and retirement planning would lose flexibility.

APPENDIX C: WHY DO WE HAVE CORPORATIONS?

Kristen makes the best pizza in town, but is reluctant to open a second location. Not because she doubts her pizza—customers are begging for another restaurant across town. She is worried that if something goes wrong at the new location, she could lose everything she owns, including her house. One lawsuit could wipe out her life savings. This concern holds back potential entrepreneurs every day, which is exactly why we need corporations.

Many people think 'corporation' is a dirty word. People generally don't talk about businesses in a negative way, just corporations. What they don't realize is that the corner bakery, the local auto repair shop and the neighborhood restaurant are likely corporations too—for very practical reasons.

Of course, all big businesses are corporations, but why are small businesses formed as corporations? Aren't small businesses just sole proprietorships (or partnerships) in which one person simply owns the business? Like Kristen's Pizza Joint—How does the corporate form help Kristen?

The corporation is one of capitalism's most important

inventions. It allows entrepreneurs to build businesses that outlast them while limiting their personal risk. The best way to think about a corporation is that it is a separate legal entity. It is distinct from the owners of the business.

There are four primary reasons that a business chooses to be a corporation:

1. Limited liability
2. Easier to raise capital
3. Employees can own stock
4. Transfer ownership easily

Limited Liability

Limited liability allows a business to take more risks than it otherwise might. Risk-taking drives progress—new products, breakthrough drugs, scientific discoveries.

Let's use Kristen's Pizza Joint as an example. If Kristen owns the restaurant personally, as a sole proprietor, she's personally liable for everything that happens there. If a customer slips and breaks their hip, a lawsuit could easily cost $200,000. If the pizza oven malfunctions and causes a fire that spreads to neighboring businesses, Kristen could face millions in damages. Even with insurance, coverage limits mean that Kristen's house, savings and other person assets are at risk. If the pizza joint is a corporation, then it is a separate legal entity. Kristen is protected. The lawsuit targets the business, not

Image by Rudy and Peter Skitterians from Pixabay

Kristen personally.

Without corporate protection, entrepreneurs like Kristen face greater risks, which limits expansion. Opening that second restaurant becomes too risky. As a corporation, Kristen can take calculated risks, open multiple locations and attract investors—who are also protected from personal liability.

Easier to Raise Capital

Being a corporation allows a business to sell shares of stock to investors. What if Kristen wanted an investor to contribute some money so she can grow her business? Perhaps she wants to have several pizza joints around the state.

Investors could purchase shares of stock from Kristen's corporation. For example, investors might invest $400,000 for 20% of the company. If Kristen owned the business as a sole proprietor, it would be difficult to bring in investors. There is no stock for investors to purchase.

What about a partnership? Investors could become partners, but then they'd be exposed to liability—exactly what investors want to avoid. If the investors wanted to be passive investors, they could structure the company as a limited partnership, but that gets more complicated. It is much simpler just to own stock.

Employees Can Own Stock

As a business grows, the company might offer shares of stock to employees as an incentive or a bonus. As a corporation, the business has shares of stock that can be given or sold to employees. This gives employees a stake in the business, aligning their interests with the company's success. Employees at successful companies have seen their stock options become quite valuable.

Easily Transfer Ownership

The ownership of a corporation can be transferred relatively easily compared to other forms of ownership. After Kristen has built a successful business, she may wish to sell the business and retire, or transfer it to her children. If the business is a corporation, then Kristen can simply sell her shares to the buyer or transfer them to her children.

Without corporations, Kristen's personal assets are always at risk. As a corporation, she is protected and can focus on building her business. That's why the corporate structure matters—it turns personal risk into manageable business risk.

APPENDIX D: MEASURING ECONOMIC FREEDOM

Economic freedom can be measured. The Fraser Institute and the Heritage Foundation have each developed indices that measure economic freedom. The indices measure 12 aspects of economic freedom. They track things such as property rights, open markets, openness to trade and investment, regulations, government size, fiscal soundness, corruption, monetary stability and taxes. They also measure the ease of starting a business.

The Fraser Institute defines economic freedom: "Economic freedom means people are allowed to make their own choices—what to produce, consume, and trade—within a framework of stable property rights, low taxes, and minimal government intervention. This environment fosters innovation, incentivizes investment, and allows for efficient allocation of resources. When entrepreneurs and firms face fewer barriers, they can respond to market demands and capitalize on opportunities, creating jobs and driving economic growth"[39]. The top five countries for economic freedom are[40]:

1. Singapore
2. Switzerland
3. Ireland
4. Taiwan
5. Luxembourg

Singapore is one of the world's most prosperous countries. It has a low rate of unemployment and its regulatory framework is business-friendly.

The United States was ranked number three in the world for economic freedom in 2000. In 2005, we were number eight. In 2020, the U.S. ranked number 17. In 2025, we came in at number 26 in economic freedom—our lowest ranking ever[41].

We are going in the wrong direction. "The major causative factor in the erosion of America's economic freedom is excessive government spending, which has resulted in mounting deficit and debt burdens over the past four years"[42].

Hong Kong led the world in economic freedom for 25 years. This year Hong Kong is not even on the list. China has been exerting heavy influence on Hong Kong and reducing its freedoms.

Hong Kong's story illustrates this perfectly. Hong Kong used to be an amazing place. Have you traveled there? Did you notice the many acres of cultivated farmland? Did you notice the oil derricks pulling up black gold from the rich oil fields? How about Hong Kong's extensive timberlands and navigable rivers? The answer is an obvious no,

---

[39] https://www.fraserinstitute.org/studies/human-freedom-index-2024

[40] https://www.heritage.org/index/pages/report

[41] The Heritage Foundation, 2025 Index of Economic Freedom, www.heritage.org/index/pages/report

[42] Ibid.

because Hong Kong does not have any of those resources. It has no natural resources at all, although it does have a well-protected harbor. Hong Kong's exceptional economic freedom led it to great economic success. No longer, unfortunately.

Russia ranked at number 131 in economic freedom. It has structural weakness, corruption and low levels of investment. The lack of economic freedom explains why it cannot turn its vast resources into a good quality of life for its people.

Venezuela ranks third to last at number 174, better only than Cuba and North Korea. This is a country with the world's largest oil reserves. Wouldn't you think that might give them a bit of an advantage?

Freedom correlates with several good outcomes. The Fraser Institute reports: "Comparing the freest 25 percent of countries with the least free[43]:

- Median earners make 5 times as much income,
- People report they are 30 percent more satisfied with their lives,
- Scientists and inventors are more productive,
- Environments are cleaner,
- Governments are less corrupt,
- People are more tolerant and charitable, and
- Extreme poverty, child mortality, and deaths from conflict are far less common."

Standards of living are much higher in countries that are economically freer, as measured by incomes per capita. In the 2024 Index, countries rated "free," "mostly free," or "moderately free" generate incomes that are more than *double* the levels in other countries and more than *three times* higher than the incomes of people living in "repressed" countries.

---

[43] https://www.fraserinstitute.org/studies/human-freedom-index-2024

The chart below from the Fraser Institute clearly expresses how economic freedom is related to income.

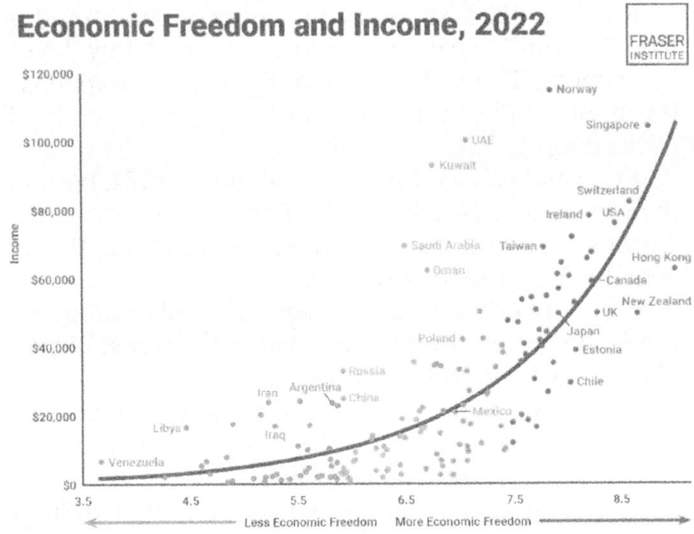

Source: Fraser Institute

The evidence confirms what theory suggests: there is a strong relationship between economic freedom and economic dynamism. When people are free to make their own choices, create businesses and engage in voluntary exchange, the results speak for themselves. Economic freedom isn't just good policy—it delivers results.

APPENDIX E: ROBOTS AND JOBS

Robots do not put people out of work, but they do change the nature of work. Factory robots, automated checkout systems, and even your car's cruise control are all forms of robots that help rather than harm employment. You probably own several robots—your dishwasher, washer and dryer are all robots. The United States has more robots in use than ever before and they make our lives better.

Every robot creates jobs. Someone has to design it, build it, program it and fix it when it breaks.

More people had jobs in the United States in 2025 than in many decades, with unemployment at just 4%[44]. We also have more robots in service than ever before. Think about that—if we have more robots than ever and more people working than ever, then robots clearly do not reduce employment. Otherwise, this would not be the

[44] U.S. Bureau of Labor Statistics, www.bls.gov/charts/employment-situation/civilian-unemployment-rate.htm

situation. The nature of the jobs may change, but robots do not reduce the number of jobs. The jobs are just different.

Image by Mane07 from Pixabay

APPENDIX F: ARTIFICIAL INTELLIGENCE

Artificial intelligence, or AI, is a powerful technology that is changing and will continue to change our lives in many ways. Many people fear that AI will eliminate their jobs, replace human workers entirely, or eventually become so powerful that it controls rather than serves humanity. Others worry about privacy and bias in decision-making.

What is Artificial Intelligence?

Artificial Intelligence refers to computer systems that can perform tasks that typically require human intelligence—like recognizing speech, solving problems, making decisions or understanding language. Instead of following pre-programmed instructions, AI systems learn from processing large amounts of data to generate decisions and responses. Think of it as teaching computers to learn and think rather than just follow commands. Today's AI can write emails, drive cars, diagnose diseases and even have conversations, though it works very differently from human intelligence.

While AI seems like a brand new invention, scientists

have actually been working on it since the mid-1950s. The recent breakthroughs in AI capability happened because of advances in computing power and access to massive amounts of data.

Robots replace physical movement or physical labor. Artificial intelligence replaces mental work or mental effort. As I noted in the last appendix, robots make our lives easier by handling repetitive physical tasks—from manufacturing cars to cleaning floors to sorting packages. But AI can handle a range of mental tasks that humans may enjoy or excel at—problem-solving, writing or analyzing. Unlike a factory robot that requires reprogramming for new tasks, AI keeps learning and improving. Eventually it will tackle increasingly sophisticated cognitive tasks. This is both exciting and unsettling.

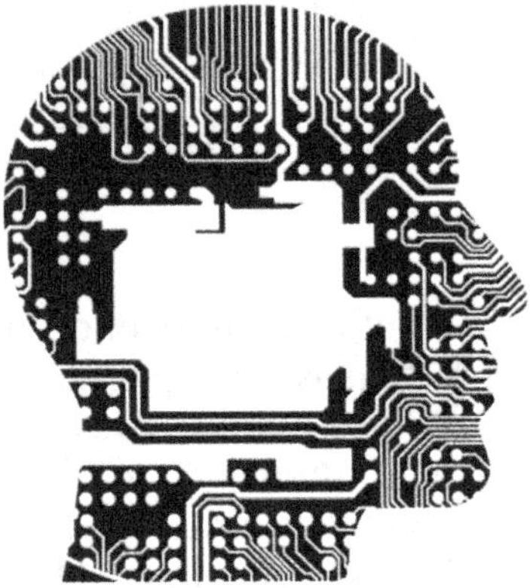

How Will AI Play Out?

Artificial intelligence shows real promise across multiple sectors. These aren't pie-in-the-sky promises—they're happening now.

AI is already making significant advances in medicine. It can accelerate drug discovery, reducing development timelines from many years to just a few years. AI is detecting cancer earlier than human doctors. We're moving toward personalized medicine based on individual genetics and virtual doctors will handle routine care around the clock.

AI is dramatically speeding up scientific research. Scientists use it to develop better batteries, find new materials and model climate solutions. The pace of innovation will accelerate as AI performs complex calculations and pattern recognition that used to take researchers years. And importantly, the cost of failure is going down.

AI makes workers more productive across many jobs. It helps lawyers research cases, helps doctors review medical scans and helps writers edit. AI isn't replacing these people—it handles the routine work so they can focus on the parts that require human judgment.

AI can also improve education. Students get AI tutors that adapt to how they learn. If a kid struggles with math, the AI figures out exactly where they're confused and adjusts its approach. It creates practice problems tailored to that student's needs. Good tutoring becomes available to anyone with internet access.

AI makes entire industries more productive and less expensive. When businesses can deliver services faster and cheaper, consumers benefit through better products and lower prices.

Most jobs will be affected by AI in some way. Where displaced workers will go is unclear—this is the first time automation has targeted mental work. But AI will likely amplify human capabilities rather than replace them and create new opportunities in ways we can't predict.

Sectors at Risk

AI will eliminate jobs across a number of employment sectors. Jobs involving repetitive, predictable and data-driven tasks will be the most at risk. Examples of sectors at risk include:

Professional & Technical:

- Software developers
- Financial analysts and accountants
- Radiologists and medical diagnosticians
- Investment advisors and portfolio managers
- Insurance underwriters and claims adjusters
- Pharmacists

Creative & Content:

- Journalists and content writers
- Copywriters and advertising creatives
- Graphic designers and illustrators
- Translators
- Video editors

A McKinsey & Company study in 2025 estimated that 20 to 30 percent of current jobs could be automated by 2030[45]. Repetitive and low-skill jobs are the most vulnerable. Sectors that have more human interaction like healthcare and education are less at risk. Despite these job displacement concerns; AI creates significant opportunities for entrepreneurs.

Entrepreneurs and AI

From the perspective of an entrepreneur, artificial intelligence is exciting and promising. Entrepreneurs will create new types of businesses made possible by AI.

Artificial intelligence will lower barriers for starting companies. It will provide tools that are affordable for new companies with limited capital. AI will enable small businesses to scale more rapidly. It will automate repetitive tasks which will enable people to focus on high-value activities like innovation.

For example, AI can write computer programs. This capability is transforming software development. New tools can generate code snippets, debug programs, and build entire applications based on natural language prompts. AI often produces functional software with minimal human oversight. It can create websites, automate business processes and develop apps.

This benefits small and large businesses by reducing the cost and complexity of software development.

[45] McKinsey & Company, www.mckinsey.com/capabilities/quantumblack/our-insights/the-state-of-ai

Prototypes can be developed faster and tested more affordably so new products can get to market faster. Non-technical entrepreneurs will be able to create specific solutions without hiring a large development team.

Opportunities for entrepreneurs include things like creating AI tools, development platforms and new types of business services, including consulting and training.

Markets will adapt. Entrepreneurs will figure out new and imaginative ways to harness AI. Based on four decades of watching entrepreneurs solve problems and create value, I can tell you that AI disruption will spawn entirely new industries—just as the internet did, as mobile technology did, and other major technological shifts have throughout history.

Summary

We don't know exactly how this will play out and we should be realistic about AI's limitations. It is impressive, but it is not always correct. Predictions can be wrong and some AI projects don't always work out as planned. AI can make mistakes, especially with unusual situations it has not seen before.

This next section explains the technology basics behind AI for interested readers.

How Does AI Act Intelligent?

Artificial intelligence generates human-like responses by analyzing massive amounts of text data and predicting the most likely next words or phrases. AI processes this information at extraordinary speed—specialized AI chips can be 2,000 times faster than typical computers at peak performance.

How does AI turn raw data into responses that seem intelligent?

1. Training on Human Patterns

AI systems dive into vast collections of text—books, articles, conversations and more. From these they learn how humans think, reason and express opinions. By analyzing patterns, the system learns to replicate the structure and style of human judgment. It produces responses that feel coherent and familiar.

2. Breaking Down Complex Questions

AI does not just retrieve information; it uses algorithms to break down questions, evaluate options and construct logical answers. It predicts the most likely response based on patterns in its training data, enabling the system to deliver coherent conclusions.

3. Sensitivity to Context

Advanced AI picks up on nuances in the questions you ask. It detects subtleties such as tone or intent. It tailors responses to be personalized and relevant, making them appear human-like.

4. Learning from Human Preferences

AI models are trained on examples of good and bad responses. Human trainers rate thousands of AI outputs, teaching the system which answers are helpful and which are not. This training helps AI learn to give responses that people actually want.

ABOUT THE AUTHOR

Thomas V. Metz, Jr. founded the boutique investment bank T.V. Metz & Co., LLC in 1983 and has been an investment banker for 42 years. The firm specialized in arranging mergers and acquisitions in the technology industries. Mr. Metz has competed transactions across North America as well as in Europe and Asia. He has arranged the sale of 78 companies. While mostly retired from active deal-making, Mr. Metz remains engaged in solving interesting and unusual business problems.

Earlier in his career he invested venture capital for a private holding company. He held positions in finance with the DeLorean Motor Company and computer sales with IBM. Mr. Metz has a B.S. degree in Mathematics and Computer Science from the University of Oregon. He holds an MBA degree from the University of California at Berkeley.

He has authored four books: *Selling the Intangible Company—How to Negotiate & Capture the Value of a Growth Firm* (John Wiley & Sons, 2009); *Perfect Your Exit Strategy—7 Steps to Maximum Value* (Bettencourt, 2016); *Defining Excellence—The Discipline of Company Definition* (Bettencourt, 2019); *Entrepreneurs: The Economic Spark* (Bettencourt, 2025).

Mr. Metz is an avid downhill skier and golfer. In his younger years he was a top nationally-ranked squash player. He is also a pilot and for many years flew his Cessna 182 named Loretta to family and golf destinations.

ACKNOWLEDGEMENTS

Many people deserve thanks for helping me clarify my ideas and improve the content and quality of the book. Their input made for a much better product.

Thanks go to Cathy Epley, who contributed her superb editing skills as well as critical thinking. I appreciate the time and effort of those who reviewed the manuscript, including Cathi Howell, Jim Noonan, Steve Bachelder, Neil Alex, Chip Arthur, Tom Maresh, Jim Palmer and Elizabeth Harrison.

I am grateful to Phil Simmons for his valuable feedback and insights on the European markets. Thanks to Pixabay, Pexels and Unsplash for allowing the use of images from their collections.

INDEX

Made in the USA
Monee, IL
04 November 2026

67387240R00105